if you're

clueless

about

accounting

and finance

and

want to

know more

SETH GODIN

PAUL LIM

Dearborn
Financial Publishing, Inc.®

If You're Clueless about Accounting and Finance and Want
to Know More

This publication is designed to provide accurate and authoritative information in regard
to the subject matter covered. It is sold with the understanding that the publisher is not
engaged in the rendering of legal, accounting, or other professional service. If legal
advice or other expert assistance is required, the services of a competent professional person should be sought.

Editorial Director: Cynthia A. Zigmund
Managing Editor: Jack Kiburz
Interior and Cover Design: Karen Engelmann

Library of Congress Cataloging-in-Publication Data
Godin, Seth
    If you're clueless about accounting and finance and want to know more / Seth
Godin, Paul Lim
        p.   cm.
    Includes index.
    ISBN 0-7931-2881-1
        1. Corporations—United States—Accounting.   2. Corporations—United States—
Finance.   I. Lim, Paul.   II. Title.
HF5686.C7G5   1998
658.15—dc21   98-5446
                                                                                CIP

Other Clueless books by Seth Godin:

If You're Clueless about Mutual Funds and Want to Know More

If You're Clueless about Retirement Planning and Want to Know More

If You're Clueless about Saving Money and Want to Know More

If You're Clueless about The Stock Market and Want to Know More

If You're Clueless about Insurance and Want to Know More

If You're Clueless about Starting Your Own Business and Want to Know More

If You're Clueless about Getting a Great Job and Want to Know More (with Beth Burns)

Acknowledgments

Thanks to Jack Kiburz and Cynthia Zigmund at Dearborn for their invaluable support and guidance, and to Karen Watts, who continues to be the evil mastermind behind the Clueless concept.

Thanks, too, go to Linda Carbone, Susan Kushnick, Theresa Cassaboon, Shelley Flannery, Rebecca Wald, and Sidney Short for their top-drawer bookmaking skills. Last, but certainly not least, we appreciate the insight and hard work of the whole crew at SGP, especially Nana Sledzieski, Lisa Lindsay, and Wendy Wax.

Contents

Chapter One: Getting a Clue about Accounting and Finance   1

Chapter Two: Getting to Know the Players   9

Chapter Three: Understanding the Language of Accounting   17

Chapter Four: Understanding the Foibles of Accounting   37

Chapter Five: Picking Up Clues from Financial Statements   55

Chapter Six: Using Key Financial Ratios   77

Chapter Seven: Understanding How Budgets Work   87

Chapter Eight: Understanding Cost Accounting   111

Chapter Nine: Managing Your Cash through the Year   123

Chapter Ten: Managing Credit without Fear   145

Chapter Eleven: Managing Your Own Inventories   155

Chapter Twelve: Understanding How Taxes Affect Your Company   169

Chapter Thirteen: Borrowing Money and Raising Capital   181

Chapter Fourteen: How the Economy Affects Your Company's Finances   193

Glossary   211

Resources   221

Index   225

GETTING
a clue
about accounting
and
FINANCE

We *all play a role in our company's finances, whether we realize it or not—even those of us who don't hold* **traditional** *finance jobs.*

For instance, if you're a sales manager or an ad manager, you can influence the speed with which your company makes its sales and converts its inventory into cash. Obviously, this has an effect on the way your company manages its finances. If sales are strong, your company may be able to build new stores, buy more goods, and hire more employees with the cash being generated from its sales. If sales are weak, it may have to borrow money or seek other forms of financing to do those things.

If you're a computer programmer or a shipping clerk, you play a role in the process, too: You influence the speed with which information and goods flow into and out of your company. If information and merchandise move faster than normal, costs are reduced. If they move slower, expenses rise. So this, too, has an impact on how your

company's finances must be managed. In fact, there isn't a single department, division, work unit, or employee who doesn't come into contact with a company's finances. Assets and liabilities, and revenues and expenses, are affected every time an employee is hired, merchandise is moved, or paperwork is pushed.

What You Do Matters

Let's say you're a sales representative at a wholesale bakery, in charge of $100 million in accounts. It takes some bakeries as long as 30 days to collect their money after all those loaves of bread and other delicacies have been delivered to their customers. Some bakeries, though, get their customers to pay up in about 25 days. If you could convince your clients to do the same, you could save your company nearly $36,000 a month, or nearly $140,000 a year.

How is that possible? Assuming that the company invests that money as soon as it collects it, the money would earn $27,800 a day for each day it was collected sooner, assuming a 10 percent annual rate of return.

Now if you could somehow persuade your customers to pay in 15 days—which some companies do—you would save the firm about $417,000.

Of course, not all of us are in charge of $100 million in accounts.

What if you just work in your company's payroll department? According to the American Institute of Certified Public Accountants, the average large American company spends $1.91 to process each weekly paycheck. Efficient companies can do it for just 36 cents per check.

Now imagine: If you could find a software program to streamline the payroll process and bring your company's costs down from $1.91 to even 50 cents a check, you could save your bosses nearly $370,000 a year, assuming you work for a company with

5,000 employees. How? By saving $1.41 per check, with 5,000 employees the company would issue 260,000 weekly paychecks a year: 260,000 x 1.41 = $366,600. In ten years, that's close to $4 million. In reality, though, your company would invest those savings each year. So, if we again assume a 10 percent annual rate of return, you would end up saving your company more than $5.8 million over the course of a decade. (Note that numbers will be rounded off for calculations in this book.)

How all this can be possible will become clear to you once you learn how your company's finances work.

What Is Finance?

Finance is the art of raising, managing, and making money in business. It's not a synonym for accounting, nor is it interchangeable with banking. However, both accounting and banking have something to do with it. Finance is a process that involves three essential steps:

- Assessing the financial performance and health of your firm

- Using that information to plan for future performance

- Executing that plan

Once a company finishes the third step—executing its plan—it goes back and *reassesses* its performance, and this *cycle of finance* repeats itself in a continuous loop. We'll explain each step throughout this book.

Just as You Affect Finance, Finance Affects You

But what if your job doesn't involve assessing your firm's finances? What if you don't take part in strategic planning? Or, what if you don't manage your own department and aren't in a position to supervise the execution of the company's plan?

You don't have to be an accountant—or have an MBA—to be affected by your company's finances. There isn't a single department in a company that finance doesn't touch.

And if you're an investor wondering whether it makes sense to plunk your money into one company versus another, you'll know how to assess their relative strengths and weaknesses by understanding the cycle of finance.

Accounting 101

Before you learn how the cycle of finance works, you have to know something about *accounting*. Sorry. There's no way to get around this. Since accounting is the *language* in which financial transactions are recorded, you've got to learn some of its vocabulary to understand what's going on.

Perhaps you're a plant manager, and your company has asked you to help rethink how the facility operates. In addition to reviewing flow charts, you may be asked to study financial statements, budgets, and reports. Even if you don't have to read these financial statements, knowing *how to* read them—and understanding the financial concepts behind them—will work to your advantage.

If you manage your company's vehicle fleet, for instance, and the company decides to lease rather than buy, you'll understand why. If you manage a work unit and find that your budget is being cut by 10 percent, you may be able to find alternative cuts to those that the division head is proposing. In fact, if you're a division head, you may be *forced* to learn this stuff, since more and more companies are demanding that individual divisions function as separate profit centers. We'll talk more about this later in the book.

In chapter 3, we'll walk you through the basics of accounting. Our intent isn't to teach you how to become an accountant—your company has an army of accountants to manage its books. Rather,

JUST IN CASE YOU WERE AFRAID TO ASK...

The term *profit* is often used interchangeably with *earnings, net income,* and even *the bottom line.* However, when people refer to the bottom line, they are often referring to profits *after* taxes. So make sure you understand what they really mean when they say profit, earnings, net income, or the bottom line.

we'll expose you to enough accounting so that you'll understand how *your company* assesses its own performance. We'll show you how companies record basic financial transactions, such as *sales* and *expenses*. And we'll show you how the routine inflow of revenues and outflow of expenses affect your company's books.

In general, accounting demands that companies record these transactions in a consistent fashion. But in some cases, companies do have latitude as to *how* they account for various assets and transactions, depending on the type of company they are, the types of assets they're dealing with, and the type of transaction being discussed. We'll explain these accounting nuances in chapter 4.

Assessing

Once you understand accounting, we'll show you how companies assess their financial health and performance—the first step in the cycle of finance. Businesses rely on three key financial statements—*the income statement, the cash flow statement, and the balance sheet*—to determine their:

FINANCIAL HISTORY

While the *balance sheet* and *income statement* evolved over hundreds of years of business, it was only after the stock market crash of 1929 and the subsequent Great Depression that the federal government began to impose many of the financial reporting standards that we're familiar with today.

In fact, the *cash flow statement* wasn't required of publicly traded companies until the 1980s.

- *Risk.* All companies want a sense not just of their short-term profits, but of their long-term survivability, or solvency. The chief tool to measure this risk is the *balance sheet*, which illustrates a company's overall financial situation—in terms of what it owns (which are its assets) and what it owes (which are its liabilities) at a given moment in time—and how much of its assets remain after it covers its liabilities.

- *Profitability.* Ultimately, companies exist not to make cars or planes or

widgets, but to generate profits. So we must always measure earnings. The chief tool for measuring this is the *income statement*.

- *Liquidity*. The economist John Maynard Keynes once noted that finance has a "fetish of liquidity." Liquidity simply refers to the ability of a company to convert its assets into cash. For many companies, liquidity can be *more* important that profits. After all, a company can be profitable 51 weeks out of the year, but if it doesn't have enough cash on hand to pay its bills on the 52nd week, it might not be able to stay in business. The chief tool to measure cash is the *cash flow statement*.

In chapter 5, we'll walk you through each of these financial statements. Then, in chapter 6, we'll show you some nifty, back-of-the-envelope equations that companies also use to gauge their health. These are called *financial ratios*.

Planning

Once your company assesses its health, it plans for the coming year. The principal blueprint your company uses to plan is called a *budget*. Companies rely on several different types of budgets: sales budgets, which project anticipated revenues for the coming year; expense budgets, which project anticipated costs; cash budgets, which project the inflow and outflow of cash; and capital budgets, which deal with large expenditures. All of these budgets accomplish the same four things:

1. They establish a company's priorities in writing.

2. They allocate resources based on those priorities and expectations.

3. They establish a company's expectations for the coming year.

4. They serve as scorecards for companies to gauge how well they are performing throughout the year compared to the expectations they had set for themselves at the beginning of the year.

We'll show you how companies prepare budgets—and budget forecasts—in chapter 7. And we'll walk you through Cost Accounting in chapter 8.

Executing

The proper execution of a financial plan involves the effective management of a company's assets, liabilities, and expenses. We'll explain how financial officers manage *cash* in chapter 9; how they manage *credit* in chapter 10; how they manage *inventories* in chapter 11; how they deal with *taxes* in chapter 12; ways they seek *financing* in chapter 13; and finally, how they handle the challenges of *macroeconomic concerns* such as inflation and interest rates in chapter 14.

Obviously, there's more to finance than this. But you're reading this book to find out how your company manages its finances, not how you yourself should. So read on, get a clue, and get an edge.

GETTING to know the PLAYERS

CHAPTER TWO

*Understanding the cycle of finance will help you figure out where you fit into your company's financial structure. You'll also figure out what the key financial players in your company **really** do. Let's take a look at what your colleagues down the hall are up to each day.*

The CFO

The top financial manager of your company is the chief financial officer, or CFO. Sometimes referred to as the vice president of finance, he reports directly to the president or chief executive officer, or CEO, who in turn reports to the board of directors and its chairman.

Technically, CFOs are equal in status to the vice president of manufacturing, vice president of engineering, and vice president of human resources. That's if you refer to a traditional corporate organizational chart.

In reality, CFOs are a company's second most important figure, just behind the

The Cycle of Finance as a Triangle

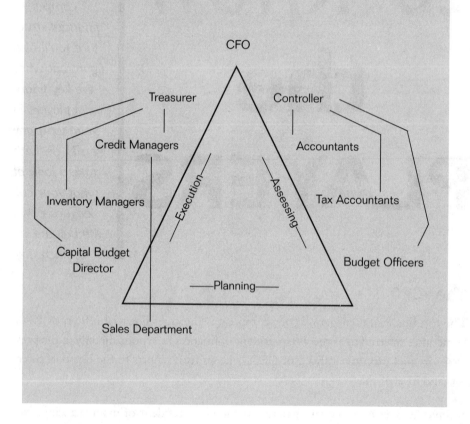

CEO. That's by virtue of the fact that they, like CEOs, have a true corporate-wide perspective. After all, CFOs oversee a company's finances—and there isn't a single department in a firm that isn't affected by finances. In recent years, the role of the CFO has greatly expanded.

"In the past, CFOs were as narrow as the columns in a ledger," Fortune magazine recently observed. *"They counted the beans and raised the bread, issuing annual reports and crunching numbers on investments proposed by somebody else. Today, the great ones are superb general managers who on top of strong financial and deal-making skills often boast a grasp of operations or a keen sense of strategy. Instead of simply measuring value, today's CFOs create it."*

It's not surprising, then, why so many of today's *CEOs* have emerged from the ranks of CFOs. Stephen Bollenbach and Doug Ivester are just two prominent examples. Before becoming CEO of Hilton Hotels, Bollenbach was CFO at Marriott in the early 1990s. There, he was credited with planning and managing the company's split into two publicly traded units—Host Marriott, a hotel management firm; and Marriott International, which owns the real estate. Bollenbach then moved on to become CFO at the Walt Disney Co., where he helped engineer the Mouse's acquisition of Capital Cities/ABC before taking the top job at Hilton.

Doug Ivester was Coca-Cola's CFO in the mid-1980s when he came up with the idea of spinning off the company's debt-ridden and sluggish bottling division, Coca-Cola Enterprises. The move got the division's debt off of Coke's books and helped Ivester land Coke's top job.

WHO'S ON THE MEASURERS' TEAM?

- Accountants
- Tax Accountants
- Cost Accountants
- Internal Auditors
- Budget Officers

The Teams

Beneath the CFO, your company's financial players are divided into two teams. Let's call them the

WHO'S ON THE MANAGERS' TEAM?

- Credit Managers

- Inventory Managers

- Plant Managers

- Capital Budgeting Staff

- Budget Officers

- Sales Staff

measurers and the *managers*. The measurers are focused on assessing and planning. The managers deal with planning and execution. When you think about it, it makes sense that both the measurers and managers share the planning function. For instance, a tax accountant (clearly a measurer) not only *assesses* the tax liability of his company; he also helps *plan* how that company can minimize taxes in the future. On the flip side, an inventory supervisor (clearly a manager) not only creates a game *plan* to control the flow of goods into and out of a warehouse, but she helps *execute* that plan.

The *measurers* are led by the company's controller and are in charge of assessing performance; accounting for assets, liabilities and costs; and planning. Team members include accountants, tax accountants, internal auditors, cost accountants (who provide managers with information pertaining to expenses related to various business activities), and budget officers.

The *managers* are led by the company's treasurer and are in charge of overseeing assets and financial planning. This team includes credit managers, inventory managers, and capital budget officers (since they oversee planning for large tangible projects).

The Controller

The controller is the chief accountant for the company. His specific duties include:

- *Selecting the firm's accounting methods.* Like any language, accounting has some foibles—one is that it allows companies to record transactions in different ways. As

FINANCIAL FACTOID

In some companies, the controller is called the *comptroller*.

Traditional Organizational Business Chart

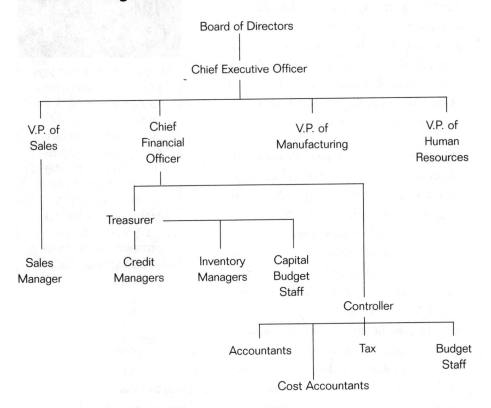

you might expect, companies tend to select those accounting methods that best suit their interests. That means they gravitate to those methods that make their assets, sales, and earnings seem larger while making their liabilities, expenses, and tax obligations seem smaller. It is the controller's job to determine which methods of accounting serve the best interests of the firm while remaining within the boundaries of acceptable practices.

- *Internal monitoring and auditing.* Once a particular accounting method is selected, the controller is in charge of enforcing that method consistently throughout the company.

- *Financial accounting.* Financial accounting refers to the periodic assess-

ment of a company's "big picture." It involves gathering financial data used to compile a company's balance sheet, income statement, and cash flow statement. This is generally done monthly, though banks and other financial services firms may do it daily. The controller is also in charge of compiling this information.

- *Managerial accounting.* To make day-to-day decisions on how to manage cash, credit, inventories, liabilities and expenses, companies often need to see the "little picture," too. In addition to information found on the balance sheet, income statement, and cash flow statement, they need to know how specific assets and divisions are performing on a perpetual basis. The process of gathering and reporting this information is called managerial accounting. That's because this information suits the purposes of managers. A typical managerial accounting report, for instance, for a grocery store chain might show how many cans of soda are being sold by stores in a particular region each day. The controller is also in charge of compiling this information.

- *Taxes.* Finally, the controller is responsible for making sure that all tax returns and payments are made on time. He also advises the CEO and CFO on tax strategy.

The Treasurer

The treasurer's job is to raise, spend, invest, and manage the company's assets. For instance, the treasurer oversees how the company:

- *Obtains financing.* All companies, regardless of their size, require financ-

---

FINANCIAL FACTOID

There's no rule that says a CFO must hold a master's degree in business administration (MBA), but most do. In fact, some MBA programs— including the prestigious Wharton School at the University of Pennsylvania—are actually geared toward training CFOs—even more so than CEOs.

ing at some point. The treasurer determines the capital needs of the company in the short, intermediate, and long term. She then decides what the most appropriate form of that financing should be, based on how much money the company needs and how much time it needs it for. If the most appropriate form of financing is debt, then the treasurer will help select the lender through which the company will obtain that financing and will negotiate the terms. If the most appropriate form of financing is equity, then the treasurer will assist the CFO to find investors for a private placement or investment banks for a public offering.

- *Manages cash.* Cash is a company's most precious asset. So, the treasurer is responsible for making sure that there's enough cash in the company's accounts at all times to meet the firm's obligations, such as payroll and taxes. That means the treasurer must ensure that bills are being collected as soon as possible and that debts are being paid on time. But there's more to it than that. The treasurer must also ensure that any excess cash is being invested properly.

- *Manages credit.* A company's credit policies often have a direct impact on its sales. For instance, a loose credit policy—in which a company extends credit to a large number of customers—tends to boost sales by giving even those consumers who don't have cash the ability to purchase their merchandise. Unfortunately, loose credit policies lead to late payments and even defaults. On the flip side, companies with tight credit policies—meaning that they extend lines of credit only to their most credit-worthy customers—forgo additional sales for the comfort of knowing that their debtors will pay their money back on time. The treasurer's job is to balance the desires of sales managers, who seek loose credit, with those of credit managers, who prefer tight policies.

FINANCIAL FACTOID

In some small companies, the CFO also serves as treasurer of the company.

- *Manages inventories.* A company that overstocks its inventory runs the risk of illiquidity by tying up its cash for long periods of time. There are, in addition, added costs associated with holding excess inventory—such as handling costs and insurance costs to guard against theft or damage. Plus, a company that understocks its inventories runs the risk of losing out on sales, by failing to provide what customers want. Based on the company's need for liquidity and profitability, the treasurer must help formulate an inventory plan.

UNDERSTANDING *the* language *of* ACCOUNTING

You don't need to be an accountant to understand how finance works. But you do need to understand some of the basic concepts of accounting—beginning with a definition of accounting itself.

Accounting is a set of rules. The rules govern how businesses record transactions, such as the sale or purchase of a product, and how they account for the things they owe and own. Though frustrating in their complexity, the rules serve an important purpose: They force businesses to measure things in a relatively *consistent* manner.

Imagine what would happen if businesses didn't conform to standard accounting practices. Let's say you work for Playtown Toys, a company that doesn't care about its accounting practices. One day, your boss asks you to compare the sales trends of the company's two divisions—its Electronic Games division and its Traditional Toys unit. You go over to the Electronics Games division and discover that revenues have grown 50 percent, thanks to a major contract it just signed with a chain of department stores to supply it with video games—next year.

17

Over at the Traditional Toys division you find that sales are flat. But upon further investigation, you learn that this division has also signed a contract with that same department store chain, in this case to supply it with thousands of units of dolls and board games. Though the value of the contract would easily boost the unit's revenues by 60 percent, this division—unlike its counterpart—decides it won't record the contract as a sale until it actually ships its products.

So which one is doing better?

Given the *inconsistent* manner in which Playtown Toys registers its sales, it is impossible to tell.

By enforcing some degree of consistency within and among companies, proper accounting allows us to compare and assess a company's health.

Managerial Accounting

As we noted in chapter 2, there are two forms of accounting: *managerial accounting* and *financial accounting*. Managerial accounting keeps track of the "little picture." It captures data on day-to-day business transactions and trends—such as product-specific sales, site-specific inventories, and divisional expenses—that company officials use to make routine decisions. For instance, the managers of Playtown Toys may want to know how many video games the company actually sold last week compared to how many it expected to sell, to help them determine whether or not to adjust their inventory.

Accountants routinely compile this data in the form of managerial reports that are distributed to various officers. If you look at the chart "Managerial Report—Week of January 1" on page 19, you'll see an example of the information that can be provided in these reports. Managerial reports are generated on an as-needed basis and are constructed to suit the needs of the managers they are intended for. Some reports are published monthly, some weekly, some even daily. While Playtown Toys may feel it sufficient to see weekly sales trends, other types of companies may desire daily updates.

Managerial Report—Week of January 1

	Actual (units)	Forecasted (units)	Actual ($)	Forecasted ($)
Video games	5,009	4,750	$125,225	$118,750
Dolls	12,998	13,000	194,970	195,000
Puzzles	406	550	3,248	4,400

Financial Accounting

Most of us are more concerned with financial accounting than managerial accounting. Financial accounting keeps track of the "big picture." It measures a company's performance—for instance, in terms of earnings and sales. These findings are published quarterly and annually in the form of income statements, balance sheets, and cash flow statements. Financial accounting thus serves several masters, not just managers. For instance, it is useful to:

- *Prospective investors*

- *The Internal Revenue Service*

- *The Securities and Exchange Commission and other government agencies*

Because outsiders require this information, too, financial accounting standards are often more rigid than managerial accounting standards. For instance, financial accounting statements must be audited. And they must conform with *generally accepted accounting principles* (GAAP).

What Is GAAP?

GAAP represents thousands of pages of rules and guidelines that the accounting profession adheres to. Some of the guidelines have evolved over centuries. Others have just recently been added—by the Financial Accounting Standards Board (FASB), the body that governs the profession.

You'll note that the first two letters of GAAP stand for *generally accepted*. Don't let that fool you. It's in the best interest of companies to comply. In fact, the IRS requires companies to conform to GAAP's conventions for the purpose of reporting taxes. And the SEC requires publicly traded companies to comply with GAAP.

One of GAAP's roles is to establish some basic concepts of accounting that all businesses follow—such as what assets are, what liabilities are, and what shareholder equity is.

The Basic Concepts of Accounting

What Is an Asset?

An asset is something of value that can be used to serve a company's needs.

Assets are broken into two categories: *fixed assets* and *current assets*. Fixed assets are those assets that will not be liquidated, or converted to cash, in the normal course of business. For many companies, that includes such items as factories and real estate. However, fixed assets do not have to be large and tangible. Intangibles like patents, copyrights, and goodwill can also be considered fixed assets. Current assets, on the other hand, are those that are intended to be converted into cash in the normal course of business, generally in under a year's time, though many current assets, such as inventory and *accounts receivable*, may be intended to be converted in three months or less. Note: Just because one company classifies an asset as *fixed* does not mean all companies must treat that same item similarly. For instance, a tractor can be considered a fixed asset to a farmer who uses it to work his land. Down the street, a farm equipment manufacturer may classify tractors as current assets, since they are a part of inventory, which will be converted into cash in the normal cycle of business.

Key Differences: Managerial vs. Financial Accounting

Managerial Accounting	Financial Accounting
Does not have to conform to GAAP	Conforms to GAAP
Purpose: To prepare management reports	Purpose: To prepare financial statements—income statement, balance sheet, and cash flow statement
Focus is on future performance	Focus is on past performance
Serves interests of management	Serves interests of investors, IRS, SEC, and management

What Is an Account Receivable?

An *account receivable* is a way for companies to keep track of money they are owed. It is made necessary by the rules of *accrual accounting*. Briefly—since we'll talk about accrual accounting in depth in chapter 4—accrual accounting states that companies can consider a product sold once they ship the merchandise. They don't have to wait until they receive payment for the goods.

For instance, let's say you work for a tool manufacturer that sells its tools to hardware stores. One day, your company delivers a $10 hammer to one of its customers. However, under a long-standing agreement, the hardware store agrees to pay you for the hammer at a later date. This is known as a *trade credit*. Even though your company hasn't been paid for the hammer, the rules of accrual accounting state that your

company ought to go ahead and register this transaction as a sale. But won't your books be out of balance until you have $10 to show for the hammer? Absolutely. So, to get around this problem, your company will establish a paper asset on its books called an account receivable to stand in for the cash it is owed until actual payment is received.

What Is a Liability?

A liability is an obligation that your company will eventually have to meet. For instance, when your company takes out a loan, it is obligated to pay that money back with interest. That's a liability. When your company hires employees, it is obligated to pay them a weekly salary. That, too, is a liability. And when it buys raw materials from its supplier, it is obligated to pay for the merchandise—another liability.

Like assets, there are two types of liabilities: *current liabilities*, which must be satisfied in less than a year; and *long-term liabilities*.

What Is an Account Payable?

An account payable is similar to the concept of an account receivable. It, too, is made necessary by accrual accounting. Under accrual accounting, a transaction occurs when your company *receives* a product—not when it pays for it. For instance, let's say you own a hardware store. You purchase a $10 hammer from your supplier, promising to pay at the end of the month. Even though you haven't spent any cash yet, accrual accounting says that a transaction has taken place and that you have *incurred a liability*. To avoid an imbalance on your books, you create a paper liability called an *account payable* representing the amount of money you owe.

ACCOUNTING ALPHABET SOUP

Over the years, different accounting bodies have been in charge of GAAP.

- *CAP*. From 1939 to 1958, the Committee on Accounting Procedure was responsible.

- *APB*. After CAP, the Accounting Principles Board took over.

- *FASB*. Since 1972, the Financial Accounting Standards Board has been in charge.

What Is Shareholder Equity?

Shareholder equity is another term to describe a company's *net worth*. A simple way to calculate a company's net worth is to take all of its assets and subtract its liabilities. In fact, this is known as the basic equation of accounting.

Net Worth = Assets − Liabilities

or

Assets = Liabilities + Net Worth

Let's say your company has $100 in assets and $50 in liabilities. It's net worth, then, would be $50 ($100 − $50 = $50). If your company has $100 in assets and $100 in liabilities, its net worth would be $0. And if it has $50 in assets and $100 in liabilities, its net worth would actually be *negative* $50.

How Companies Account for Assets, Liabilities, and Net Worth

Companies keep track of their assets, liabilities, and net worth in several steps. First, they maintain a running list of transactions as they occur— much like a diary or a journal (though these days this is done on computer). At the same time, they maintain separate ledgers, or accounts, for each category of their assets and liabilities. So, for instance, your company might have separate accounts to keep track of its cash, inventories, and accounts receivable. On the liability side, your

CURRENT VS. NONCURRENT

A *current asset* is one that is intended to be converted to cash in the normal operation of business—generally within a year, such as inventory. A *noncurrent* asset is one that is not intended to be converted to cash in the normal operation of business. For many companies, examples of noncurrent assets include equipment and property. Similarly, a *current liability* is one that will come due in less than a year, such as salary and wages. And a *noncurrent* liability is a long-term obligation. It is generally called a *long-term liability* or *other liabilities* or by specific names, such as deferred taxes or bank loans.

company may maintain separate accounts for such things as wages payable and accounts payable. Every time your company sells something or buys something, it records it in its running journal. Next, it posts, or transcribes, that same information to the affected accounts. And your company will also transcribe the activity that has taken place in its individual accounts onto a *general ledger*, a master account that combines the results of all its individual accounts. The general ledger is what we refer to when we talk about a company's "books." If you look at the "General Ledger" chart on page 25, you'll see what a portion of a general ledger might look like. As they post transactions to the various accounts, accountants rely on something called a T-account to explain just what is going on. A T-account is a visual aid of sorts. It's a chart with two columns—one on the left side of the T and one on the right. You can see what a T-account looks like in the example below. T-accounts help explain the *double-entry system* of accounting that businesses use—we'll explain both in a second.

THE THREE KEY TERMS OF ACCOUNTING

- *Assets.* An asset is a resource owned by a company.

- *Liabilities.* A liability is a debt the company owes. Companies must often take on debt, or liabilities, to acquire assets.

- *Shareholder equity.* This is the investment the company's shareholders have sunk into the firm. This is another source of funds to acquire assets.

T-Account

	Debit	Credit
Asset:		
Accounts Receivable		

Double-Entry Accounting

What is double-entry accounting and how does it work? Let's say you go out and buy a television set for your personal use. For the sake of argument, let's assume that you write out a check for $500 to purchase the set. To record this transaction, all you would do is subtract $500 from the listed balance in your checkbook.

General Ledger

	Starting Balance	January	February	March	April	May	June	Mid-year Balance
Asset Accounts:								
Accounts Receivable	$20,000	$550	$(1,000)	$5,000	$(900)	$4,000	$500	$28,150
Cash	10,000	300		(500)	300	1,000	(200)	10,900
Inventories	40,000	10,000		(4,000)			(3,000)	43,000
Liability Accounts:								
Accounts Payable	10,000	400	(600)	1,000	(2,000)	1,000	500	10,300
Wages Payable	20,000	1,000	(1,000)	2,000	(500)	2,000	(4,000)	19,500

If a company were to purchase that television set, it, too, would subtract $500 from its checking account. However, it would also *add* the value of the television—$500— to another account. That account might be called *office equipment* or *inventory*. The *double-entry* accounting system gets its name from this second step.

Why do businesses do this? Simple: This second step in double-entry accounting ensures that transactions are recorded accurately. How? All we have to do is plug in the changes to our original equation: Assets – Liabilities = Net Worth, or put another way, Assets = Liabilities + Net Worth. Assume that at the start of our transaction our net worth was $2,000. That's based on $1,000 in liabilities and $3,000 in assets.

$3,000 (assets) = $1,000 (liabilities) + $2,000 (net worth)

If we were simply to subtract that $500 from our checkbook, our equation might look like this:

$2,500 (assets) = $1,000 (liabilities) + $2,000 (net worth)

The Fundamental Equation of Accounting

The principal equation of accounting boils down to this: **Assets = Liabilities + Shareholder Equity.**

Anything that affects one side of this equation affects the other side. For instance, let's say your company generates $100 in revenues. *Revenue* represents an increase in assets from operations. But because assets are rising, so, too, must shareholder equity to balance this equation. Similarly, an *expense* represents a decrease in assets through operations or an increase in liabilities. If assets are decreasing while liabilities are increasing, then shareholder equity must go down as expenses are incurred to balance the equation.

However, now, the equation does *not* balance. This tells us something is wrong. Obviously, though paying for the television expended one type of asset—cash—it added another type of asset to our holdings. The television being worth $500, we can add it to our equation:

$3,000 (assets) = $1,000 (liabilities) + $2,000 (net worth)

Remember: Unlike individuals, companies are obligated to maintain records of their assets, liabilities, and net worth.

Double-Entry Accounting and T-Accounts

Now that you understand the principles of double-entry accounting, let's see how companies physically record transactions in their ledgers, using T-accounts.

To begin with, look at the example of a "T-Account" again. You'll notice that the left side of the T account is labeled *debit*. And the right side is called *credit*. Most of us associate the term *credit* with something positive and *debit* with something negative. After all, when something is credited to our checking account, the account grows. When we use a debit card, money is subtracted from our account. But for the purposes of accounting, forget those conventions. A debit is simply the left side of the T-account and a credit is simply the right.

The rules of posting a transaction to a T-account are straightforward. When a transaction adds value to an asset account, the company *debits* that amount. All that means is that the amount of the additional value is written down on the left side of the T. When a transaction reduces the value of an asset account, the amount is *credited*, or written down on the right side of the T. Conversely, if a transaction adds to a liability or net worth account, it is *credited*. Once again, that means that amount of the transaction is written down on the right-hand side of the T. And if a transaction reduces the value of a liability or net worth account, that amount is *debited*. Note: You may be wondering how a net worth account can change. Expenses and the issuance of dividends, for instance, reduce net worth and are therefore debited. Revenues add to net worth, and therefore are credited. Once you memorize these rules—and get over any confusion you have with debits and credits—posting transactions to a T is quite simple.

Let's go back to the example of the television and use the T-accounts on the following page to show how this transaction would be recorded. Let's say your company begins the day with $11,000 in assets; $1,000 of that is in the form

WHAT TO DEBIT AND WHAT TO CREDIT

Don't even try to understand why some transactions are debited and others credited to ledger accounts. Just remember that:

- An *increase in assets* is recorded as a debit.

- A *decrease in assets* is recorded as a credit.

- An *increase in liabilities or net worth* is recorded as a credit.

- A *decrease in liabilities or net worth* is recorded as a debit.

of cash. The remaining $10,000 is in the form of office equipment. During the day, your company buys a television set. It spends $500 in cash. Since cash is an asset and since you're subtracting from it, you *credit* this account.

	Debit	Credit	
Asset:			
Cash	$1,000		Beginning Balance
		$500	Transaction 1
	$500		Current Balance

	Debit	Credit	
Asset:			
Office Equipment	$10,000		Beginning Balance
	$500		Transaction 1
	$10,500		Current Balance

Double-entry accounting, however, requires your company to account for the value of the television, as well. It does so in a ledger called office equipment. Since office equipment is an asset, and since it is increasing, you *debit* this T-account $500.

At the end of the day, your company takes stock of its assets. By looking at its T-accounts, the company concludes it still has $11,000 in assets. However, instead of $1,000 in cash and $10,000 in office equipment, it now has $500 in cash and $10,500 in office equipment.

How Accounting Works in the Real World

Now that you know how T-accounts work, let's see how a typical series of business transactions in an *operating cycle* affects a company's asset and liability accounts.

Step 1: A Company Buys Raw Materials

Let's assume you work for Playtown Toys. Like all manufacturers, the company needs raw materials to make its products. So it buys $100 worth of wood and plastic from its supplier. Playtown pays for this on credit. It takes delivery of the supplies and promises to pay the supplier back at a later date. When a company does this, you'll recall, it establishes an *account payable*, which is a liability account.

Because Playtown is increasing a liability account, it must *credit* accounts payable by $100.

At the same time, the company takes possession of $100 worth of raw materials, which goes into its inventories. Inventory is an asset, so the accountants must *debit* this account by $100.

	Debit	Credit	
Liability:			
Accounts Payable		$0	Beginning Balance
		$100	Transaction 1

	Debit	Credit	
Asset:			
Inventory	$0		Beginning Balance
	$100		Transaction 1

Step 2: The Company Makes Its Products

Playtown converts the raw materials into toys, which are then warehoused in its facilities. The conversion process costs the company $100. This adds to the value of inventory, which went from raw materials to finished goods. So we debit inventory $100.

On the other side of the ledger, Playtown owes its employees for the labor it took to make the toys. Since it won't issue paychecks for another week or two, it establishes a liability account called *wages payable*. Since it is adding to this liability, it credits this account.

	Debit	**Credit**	
Asset:			
Inventory	$0		Beginning Balance
	$100		Transaction 1
	$100		Transaction 2

	Debit	**Credit**	
Liability:			
Wages Payable		$0	Beginning Balance
		$100	Transaction 1

Step 3: The Company Sells Products

A department store has agreed to buy the company's total inventory of toys for $300. Playtown ships the toys and books the sale.

Since the store hasn't paid for the toys yet, Playtown sets up an *account receivable* worth $300. An account receivable is an asset and Playtown is adding to this asset, so it debits the account $300.

At the same time, Playtown must account for the loss of inventory. A reduction in an asset account must be credited, so Playtown credits its inventory ledger $200. (Notice, the company credits the account $200—the amount of money it cost to produce the toys, not the actual selling price.)

	Debit	**Credit**	
Asset:			
Accounts Receivable	$0		Beginning Balance
	$300		Transaction 1

	Debit	**Credit**	
Asset:			
Inventory	$0		Beginning Balance
	$100		Transaction 1
	$100		Transaction 2
		$200	Transaction 3

Step 4: The Company Pays Bills

The toy company still owes its supplier $100 for the raw materials from Step 1. So it takes $100 in cash out of its checking account and uses it to pay off its account payable—a liability. That means it credits cash and debits accounts payable.

	Debit	**Credit**	
Asset:			
Cash	$0		Beginning Balance
		$100	Transaction 1

	Debit	**Credit**	
Liability:			
Accounts Payable		$0	Beginning Balance
		$100	Transaction 1
	$100		Transaction 2

Step 5: The Company Collects Bills

The company receives payment from the department store for the toys it shipped. This means Playtown adds $300 to its account called cash (which it debits) and subtracts $300 from its asset account called accounts receivable (which it credits).

	Debit	**Credit**	
Asset:			
Cash	$0		Beginning Balance
		$100	Transaction 1
	$300		Transaction 2

	Debit	Credit	
Liability:			
Accounts Receivable	$0		Beginning Balance
	$300		Transaction 1
		$300	Transaction 2

Step 6: The Company Pays Its Workers

Finally, Playtown takes $100 out of its cash account to pay its workers the money they are owed. This reduces its cash account and reduces its liability account. This means it credits cash $100 and debits wages payable $100.

	Debit	Credit	
Asset:			
Cash	$0		Beginning Balance
		$100	Transaction 1
	$300		Transaction 2
		$100	Transaction 3

	Debit	Credit	
Liability:			
Wages Payable		$0	Beginning Balance
		$100	Transaction 1
	$100		Transaction 2

Step 7: The Company Tallies the Accounts

The company can now calculate its accounts. After seven steps, Playtown Toys discovers that it has zeroed out both its accounts payable and accounts receivable. In fact, it has zeroed out every account except for cash, which shows a $100 debit. This represents the company's recorded profit.

Asset Accounts:

	Debit	Credit	
Accounts Receivable	$0		Beginning Balance
	$300		Transaction 1
		$300	Transaction 2
	$0		End Balance

	Debit	Credit	
Cash	$0		Beginning Balance
		$100	Transaction 1
	$300		Transaction 2
		$100	Transaction 3
	$100		End Balance

	Debit	Credit	
Inventory	$0		Beginning Balance
	$100		Transaction 1
	$100		Transaction 2
		$200	Transaction 3
	$0		End Balance

Liability Accounts:

	Debit	Credit	
Accounts Payable		$0	Beginning Balance
		$100	Transaction 1
	$100		Transaction 2
		$0	End Balance

	Debit	Credit	
Wages Payable		$0	Beginning Balance
		$100	Transaction 1
	$100		Transaction 2
		$0	End Balance

There. See how easy that was?

UNDERSTANDING *the* foibles *of* ACCOUNTING

CHAPTER FOUR

So why is it that the rules of accounting demand **consistency,** and not **uniformity?** Wouldn't a uniform accounting system allow you to compare and assess companies that much more accurately?

Well, the problem is that an absolutely uniform system of accounting would not reflect the unique nature of different types of businesses. And in that sense, uniformity may be not only inaccurate but unfair.

Is it fair, for instance, for a steel manufacturer—which is constantly investing in heavy machinery—to account for those purchases the same way a service-oriented company like a restaurant accounts for pots and pans? Of course not. The heavy machinery could last 20 years, while the pots and pans may only survive two years. Would it be fair for a computer company to value its assets the same way a jeweler does? Of course not. The computer maker's inventory of PCs tends to lose value every day as

37

technology becomes obsolete, while the jeweler's inventory of diamonds and precious metals tends to appreciate in value over time.

To be fair, then, the rules of accounting sometimes allow companies to record transactions and assets in different ways—provided that those accounting methods remain consistent within the company and over time.

In general, there is a degree of flexibility in determining:

- *When* transactions are recorded

- *How* inventory is valued

- *How* other assets are valued

- *How* the devaluation or depreciation of assets is recorded

When Is a Transaction a Transaction?

Determining when to record a transaction is vital to the accounting process. If companies were allowed to record 1997 sales in 1998, for instance, it would be impossible to judge how well a company was doing one year versus the next. But forcing all companies to account for sales in the same manner is just as unfair. That's why there are two basic accounting methods to determine when a transaction must be recorded.

Method 1: When Cash Changes Hands

When you go to the store to buy groceries, at what point do you say that a transaction has been made?

a. When you pick out the produce and canned goods you want and place them into your cart?

b. When you leave the store and load the groceries into your car?

c. When you hand over the money to the cashier?

Obviously, the answer is *c*. A sale has been transacted at the moment when the customer pays the company—in this case the supermarket—for its goods.

This concept of accounting for sales is called *cash basis accounting*. Most of us understand it because it is the system we use when we balance our checkbook. When we buy a stereo, for instance, we subtract the amount of the stereo from our checkbook only *after* we give the check to the store. When we go to the ATM to withdraw cash—which is also a transaction—we record it in our checkbook only *after* the machine spits out the money. In other words, we don't record the fact that a transaction has occurred until *after* payment is made.

Similarly, when a company uses the cash accounting system, it records a sale only after it receives payment from customers, and it records expenses only after it actually pays its suppliers.

As simple as cash accounting is, though, it has its shortcomings, which is why few companies—really only those that don't rely on credit accounts—actually use cash accounting to record transactions in their ledgers.

Let's go back to our example of the grocery store. These days, some of us pay for our groceries with a credit card. This raises an interesting question. When our credit card is swiped, are we actually paying for the groceries ourselves? No. The bank or credit union that issues the credit card pays the grocery store, and we promise to pay the bank back within 30 days. The grocery store can record this as a transaction because it has received payment from someone for the goods it handed over. But should you record this as a transaction in your checkbook? It's unclear.

Businesses run into a similar dilemma. When an auto repair shop, for instance, buys mufflers from a parts dealer, it doesn't pay cash on delivery. Instead, it promises to pay the parts dealer for the goods delivered within a reasonable amount of time—generally, within 30 to 60 days, just like a credit card. But should it wait for 30 to 60 days to record the transaction, or should it record the transaction right now?

Method 2: When Goods and Services Are Delivered

To avoid the problems of cash accounting, most businesses—especially those that must rely on credit to conduct business—use a different method to determine when transactions must be recorded: *accrual basis accounting*.

With accrual accounting, a company records a transaction not when payment has been made, but when services or goods have been delivered. So in our example, the parts dealer would record the *delivery* of its mufflers to the auto repair shop as a sale on its books.

But not all companies conduct business this way. Law firms, for instance, don't render their services in one fell swoop. Legal services tend to drag out—at least until a specific case is resolved or when a retainer contract expires. Accrual accounting recognizes this nuance. It says that a sale can also be registered the moment a customer and a company have entered into a legal obligation.

The same rules apply when recording expenses. When a company receives a shipment of goods from its suppliers—or enters into a legal contract to do so—it immediately records this as a transaction on T-accounts in its ledgers.

Accrual accounting adds a level of complexity that cash accounting avoids. For instance, under accrual accounting, businesses must establish paper assets and liabilities known as accounts receivable and accounts payable to make sure that their books are balanced while waiting to receive or make payments, as explained in chapter 3.

But accrual accounting is infinitely more fair and accurate—in terms of reflecting what is taking place during a business cycle.

For instance, what if a parts dealer delivers its goods to an auto repair shop at the end of one year but doesn't receive payment until the beginning of the next? Under cash accounting, the company's income statement would be understated in Year 1, since its inventories would have been depleted. And in Year 2, it would be overstated because the company's books would show an influx of cash based on a sale it transacted the previous year. Accrual accounting avoids this problem by establishing accounts receivable and accounts payable to temporarily balance the books.

How Do You Measure Inventories?

Valuing inventory is a critical task. How companies value their inventories could mean the difference between recording a profit in a given year and reporting a loss. That's because inventory costs contribute to the total cost of bringing a product to market.

Unfortunately, a uniform accounting system would force some companies to overvalue their inventories, which could lead to a loss, while forcing others to undervalue their inventories, leading to inflated profits. That's why there's more than one way to account for inventories.

Method 1: First In, First Out

Let's say you're a retailer with ten Tickle Me Elmo dolls in inventory. You purchased the first doll a year ago from your supplier for $25. You bought the tenth doll just this week, for $30. When you turn around and sell a doll to a customer, which one do you sell? Do you sell the first one, which cost you $25, or the tenth, which cost you $30? Or one in between?

As the name indicates, the First In, First Out method (abbreviated as FIFO) assumes that the company sells the first product it put into inventory. In our example, you'd sell the $25 doll. (Your company can actually sell whichever doll it wants. It simply assumes that it sold a doll that cost $25.) If your customer is willing to pay $50 for the doll, you'd clear a $25 profit.

Had you used the Last In, First Out (LIFO) method, though, you would assume that the last doll put into inventory would be the first one sold. In that case, you would have cleared just $20.

Not only does FIFO tend to inflate profits—because thanks to inflation, products put into inventory last often cost more than products put in first—FIFO also leaves companies with a greater remaining inventory asset value. (You sold the cheaper doll and left the more expensive one in inventory. Hence, your inventory is worth more.)

Companies that are especially concerned with short-term profitability benefit from FIFO. So, too, do those that want to demonstrate asset size—such as start-up firms that need to prove their stability to would-be investors.

Method 2: Last In, First Out

Why don't all companies rely on FIFO, if in fact those that do tend to report greater profits and greater inventory assets?

For starters, not all companies report greater profits with FIFO. An example may be a computer maker, for whom the cost of building the first computer may have been *more* than the cost of building the last. After all, as technology blossoms, the cost of manufacturing that technology tends to fall.

Furthermore, LIFO offers a more accurate view of a company's inventory picture, especially in high inflationary times. So companies in highly competitive industries that need to make absolutely sure that their inventory and pricing policies are correct may benefit from LIFO. In fact, companies whose goods are impacted by inflation are better off with LIFO, as it gives a truer picture of profitability in inflationary times.

Consider this: When inflation is high, as it was in the early 1980s, the spread between the cost of the first item put into inventory and the last tends to be great. For instance, let's say you're selling basketballs. The first basketball you bought cost $10. But inflation has been running so high that the last basketball bought and put into inventory cost $20. If you turned around and sold a basketball for $25, you'd clear $15 under FIFO.

	FIFO Method	LIFO Method
Sales	$50	$50
Inventory Costs	(25)	(30)
Gross Profit	$25	$20

Accrual Basis Accounting vs. Cash Basis Accounting

	Accrual Basis	Cash Basis
Recognizes sale once...	Products Shipped	Payment Received
Recognizes expense once...	Goods Received	Payment Sent

If you sold it under LIFO, you'd clear only $5. But by relying on LIFO, you'd come to a quicker realization that inflation was severely impacting your profit margin. That additional information may help you decide to raise the price of your basketballs to $35.

Companies that want to reduce taxes may find LIFO more useful, as well. For instance, let's go back to the example of the basketballs. By using FIFO, you cleared $10 more in profit. That's the good news. But there's also some corresponding bad news: You have to pay taxes on your profits. If your company is taxed at a rate of, say, 30 percent, you'd owe the IRS $4.50 per ball under FIFO. But under LIFO, your debt to Uncle Sam would only be one-third as much, or $1.50. If you sold 1,000 basketballs, you'd enjoy $10,000 more in profits but you'd owe $3,000 more in taxes—which might be due immediately. Therefore, for companies that run into routine cash flow problems—such as retailers or cyclical industrial companies—LIFO may be a better bet, despite its lower profits.

WHY USE FIFO?

- More profitability

- Greater value assessed to remaining inventory

Profits and Taxes: FIFO vs. LIFO

	FIFO Method	LIFO Method
Sales	$25,000	$25,000
Inventory Cost	(10,000)	(20,000)
Gross Profit	$15,000	$5,000

Warning: Not all companies can use LIFO. The IRS, for instance, will not allow a service company to use LIFO. Also, once you switch from FIFO to LIFO, the IRS probably won't let you switch back.

How Do You Measure an Asset?

Method 1: Historic Cost

When it comes to a company's financial statements, GAAP requires the use of *historic cost* valuation. All this means is that the company's accountants are forced to record on the books the original cost of the asset. For instance, let's say your company owns a five-year-old truck. Under the historic cost method, it would value the truck based on the price it paid five years ago. Let's assume it cost $20,000 back then.

This $20,000 is the amount that your company will use when calculating the depreciation value of that truck. (We'll get to depreciation in a moment.)

WHY USE LIFO?

- Lower taxes
- Greater cash flow
- More accuracy

Though GAAP requires historic cost valuation for financial statement purposes, there's nothing to stop management from assessing its asset base differently for its managerial reports or shareholder reports. Therefore, companies may rely on three other methods of asset valuation.

Method 2: Current Cost

Using this method, a company would value an asset based on what it thinks it's worth now. Of

Two Other Inventory Valuation Methods

In addition to LIFO and FIFO, companies can rely on two other inventory costing methods. They are:

- *Specific identification.* The most accurate way to value inventory is to actually record how much it cost your company to produce each of the products in its inventory. Unfortunately, the vast majority of companies cannot rely on this method, for logistical reasons. For instance, imagine the nightmare a large music store would have keeping track of the cost of each of the thousands of compact discs, cassettes, and albums it has in stock. On the other hand, some businesses are capable of using specific identification. A jeweler with ten diamond necklaces in stock, for example, can easily record the cost of each item in its inventory.

- *Weighted average.* The weighted average system represents the antithesis of specific identification. Specific identification assumes each product in inventory is unique. Weighted average assumes the opposite. For instance, let's say yours is a hardware store, which maintains tens of thousands of nails and bolts and screws in large bins. The first 7,500 nails could have cost your firm 2 cents a piece. The next 10,000 could have cost 3 cents. And the remaining 2,500 could have cost 4 cents. But once all the nails get thrown in a bin, how can you tell which nails came from the first, second, or third batch? Under the weighted average system, a company can simply add up the total costs of a particular type of product in its inventory and divide them by how many units of that product are in stock.

course, unlike the historic cost—which was actually negotiated in the marketplace between a buyer and a seller—this is a judgment call.

Method 3: Exit Cost

Using this method, a company would value an asset based on what it could get for it if it liquidated that asset right now. In our example, the company might believe the truck is currently worth $10,000. But if it can get only $8,000 for it, the exit-cost value of that truck will be $8,000.

Method 4: Replacement Cost

If an asset were stolen, the company would have to buy a new one to replace it. So some companies believe it's fair to value the old asset based on what it would cost now to replace it.

If new trucks go for $30,000, for instance, the company in our example would value its truck at $30,000, despite the fact that it's five years old.

So you can see that the value of an identical asset can differ wildly—in our example, a five-year-old truck can be worth anywhere from $8,000 to $30,000—depending on which accounting method the company relies on.

How Do You Account for an Asset's Gradual Loss in Value?

You've probably heard of the term *depreciation*. But what does it mean? When an asset *depreciates*, it loses value. It's as simple as that.

Most assets, at one point or another, lose value over their useful life. Consider a car. You may have bought a car for $20,000 five years ago, but the moment you drove it off the lot, its value dropped to $15,000. The moment you put 30,000 miles on the odometer, the car's value may have dropped another $5,000. Eventually, once the engine blows out, the car may be reduced to a mere $200 in value.

Similarly, the buildings, equipment, and machinery that a company invests in lose value. (Alternatively, land tends to appreciate in value. Also land, unlike buildings and machinery, has a potentially infinite lifespan and, therefore, is not depreciated.) The rules of accounting don't always enforce uniform ways to measure that devaluation, since different assets at different companies lose their usefulness over different periods of time—for instance, depending on usage.

For instance, let's say you work for a taxicab company. The company pays $20,000 to buy a new taxicab this year. But it plans to use that car for the next seven years. Is it fair for the company's books to record all $20,000 of expenses in Year 1, when Years 2–7 will also benefit from the asset? Of course not. The financial statements for Years 2–7 should also reflect the shared burden of paying for the asset. (Otherwise, companies could jigger their books simply by accounting for asset purchases up front, making subsequent years look rosy.)

The rules of accounting do this by making companies *expense* the value that an asset loses each year on that year's income statement.

If that $20,000 taxicab loses an equal amount of its value each year over seven years, the company would depreciate $2,857 a year. So, in every year's income statement over the next seven years, the company would allocate $2,857 worth of expenses against its profits. You'll see how this works in chapter 5, when we discuss financial statements.

But how should a company keep track of how its assets are losing value?

DEPRECIATION BY ANY OTHER NAME...

A term similar to depreciation is *amortization.* Depreciation generally refers to the gradual reduction in value of *tangible fixed assets,* such as buildings and facilities. When a company does the same with *intangible fixed assets,* such as patents, copyrights, or goodwill, the company amortizes those assets. Under GAAP, though, a company must generally use the *straight-line* method to amortize its intangible assets.

Method 1: Straight-Line Depreciation

Straight-line depreciation works just like the taxicab example. A company divides the life of its asset—often dictated by the IRS—into the historic price of the asset, and then depreciates that sum equally over its life expectancy. For example, imagine you work for a newspaper company with a printing press with a ten-year life span. Assuming the company paid $1 million for the equipment, it divides $1 million by ten years, which equals $100,000. That means the company believes the press is depreciating in value $100,000 each year for the next ten years.

But what if the ABC Newspaper Co.'s presses last more than ten years? That's possible, since the ten-year projection was just an educated guess. If the asset outlives its lifespan, ABC Newspaper Co. must still stop depreciating the asset at Year 10. If the printing press peters out in Year 5, the company may choose to sell the asset or write it off its books.

Straight-Line Depreciation for ABC Newspaper Company

	Amount depreciated and expensed to the income statement each year	Remaining value of $1 million printing press at end of year
Year 1	$100,000	$900,000
Year 2	100,000	800,000
Year 3	100,000	700,000
Year 4	100,000	600,000
Year 5	100,000	500,000
Year 6	100,000	400,000
Year 7	100,000	300,000
Year 8	100,000	200,000
Year 9	100,000	100,000
Year 10	100,000	0

Method 2: Accelerated Depreciation

Though it's a neat and clean method of accounting, not all companies rely on straight-line depreciation. That's because not all assets lose value evenly over the years. In fact, most assets tend to lose the majority of their value in the early years. Accountants call this *accelerated depreciation.*

There are three basic methods for calculating accelerated depreciation, listed below. But beware: Because accelerated depreciation methods reflect greater depreciation in the early years, companies will be forced to expense greater amounts early on, which will hurt their profits early on.

Also, once a company chooses one method—or if the IRS assigns a method—it must stick with it for the life of the asset.

The 200 Percent Method

Some refer to this method as the *double-declining balance* approach.

Let's go back to the newspaper company example. The ABC Newspaper Co.'s printing press has an anicipated life span of ten years.

Under straight-line depreciation, the company divides $1 million—the historic cost of its printing press—by ten to arrive at $100,000. It depreciates this amount—ten percent—every year for ten years.

Under the double-declining balance method you depreciate double that amount—20 percent. However, you depreciate that 20 percent off the *remaining* or *declining* value of the asset—not the original value. For instance, in Year 1, the value of the printing press is the full $1 million. Twenty percent of $1 million is $200,000—and that's how much of the asset you depreciate in that year. In Year 2, the remaining value of the press is $800,000. So you take 20 percent of $800,000 and you get $160,000. In Year 3, the remaining value of the press is $640,000. So you take 20 percent of that—$128,000—and depreciate that amoumt.

At the end of Year 10, you'll notice that the printing press still has a value of $107,374. The company would simply depreciate that off, in addition to its scheduled $26,844.

200 Percent Depreciation for ABC Newspaper Company

	Amount depreciated and expensed to the income statement each year	Remaining value of $1 million printing press at end of year
Year 1	$200,000	$800,000
Year 2	160,000	640,000
Year 3	128,000	512,000
Year 4	102,400	409,600
Year 5	81,920	327,680
Year 6	65,536	262,144
Year 7	52,429	209,715
Year 8	41,943	167,772
Year 9	33,554	134,218
Year 10	26,844 + remaining	0
	107,374	

The 150 Percent Rule

The 150 percent rule works just like the 200 percent rule, except that (in our example) instead of depreciating 20 percent of the asset's remaining value, you would depreciate 15 percent.

Here again, in Year 10, the company would not only depreciate the scheduled $34,742, but also the $196,874 left over.

The Sum-of-the-Years Rule

This is another accelerated depreciation method. Like the other methods, companies that use this method must first determine the anticipated life span of their asset.

Let's go back to the ABC Newspaper Co. ABC's press has a life span of ten years. Under the sum-of-the-years rule, the company would add up all the numbers of the years for which the printing press will be useful or the number of years the IRS deems it useful. This gives us 55 (1+2+3+4+5+6+7+8+9+10 = 55).

150 Percent Depreciation for ABC Newspaper Company

	Amount depreciated and expensed to the income statement each year	Remaining value of $1 million printing press at end of year
Year 1	$150,000	$850,000
Year 2	127,500	722,500
Year 3	108,375	614,125
Year 4	92,119	522,006
Year 5	78,301	443,705
Year 6	66,556	377,149
Year 7	56,572	320,577
Year 8	48,087	272,490
Year 9	40,874	231,616
Year 10	34,742 + remaining 196,874	0

In Year 1, the company would multiply the historic cost of the asset, $1 million, by 10/55. In Year 2, the company would multiply the historic cost of the press by 9/55. In Year 3, it would multiply the historic cost by 8/55, and so on. (Notice, you keep multiplying by the *original cost* under this method, not a reduced value.)

You'll notice that like the straight-line method, sum-of-the-years is a clean way to depreciate away the entire amount of the asset during its life span.

Now let's compare all four methods. Notice that midway through the life expectancy of the printing press, the *sum-of-the-years* method depreciated nearly three-quarters of its value away; the *200 percent* method depreciated more than two-thirds of the value; the *150 percent* method depreciated away more than half; while the *straight-line* method accounted for exactly half.

If the ABC Newspaper Co. used the *sum-of-the-years* method, its expenses would have been $227,273 more in the first five years than they would have been under the *straight-line* method. And that would have come directly out of profits. But in the last five years, the ABC Newspaper Co. would have had $227,273 *less* depreciation expenses than under *straight-line* depreciation method.

Sum-of-the-Years Depreciation for
ABC Newspaper Company

	Amount depreciated and expensed to the income statement each year	Remaining value of $1 million printing press at end of year
Year 1	$181,818	$818,182
Year 2	163,636	654,546
Year 3	145,455	509,091
Year 4	127,273	381,818
Year 5	109,091	272,727
Year 6	90,909	181,818
Year 7	72,727	109,091
Year 8	54,545	54,546
Year 9	36,364	18,182
Year 10	18,182	0

Companies should select the most appropriate depreciation method based on the specific asset and how it tends to lose value. Many companies will do this for their official tax-reporting purposes. However, they might simultaneously show shareholders a separate set of numbers. For instance, they may choose to depreciate their assets under the sum-of-the-years method and report that to the IRS. But their shareholders may get a separate set of numbers generated under the straight-line method, since it reflects lower expenses—and greater profits—in the first few years of major asset purchases. Unfortunately, GAAP allows for this discrepancy. However, companies must adhere to one consistent method of depreciation for the purposes of maintaining records on their financial statements over time. We discuss these financial statements in the following chapter.

Comparing the Depreciation Methods

	Sum-of-the-Years	200 Percent Method	150 Percent Method	Straight-Line Method
Year 1	$181,818	$200,000	$150,000	$100,000
Year 2	163,636	160,000	127,500	100,000
Year 3	145,455	128,000	108,375	100,000
Year 4	127,273	102,400	92,119	100,000
Year 5	109,091	81,920	78,301	100,000
Total depreciation after five years	$727,273	$672,320	$556,295	$500,000
Year 6	$90,909	$65,536	$66,556	$100,000
Year 7	72,727	52,429	56,572	100,000
Year 8	54,545	41,943	48,087	100,000
Year 9	36,364	33,554	40,874	100,000
Year 10	18,182	134,218	231,616	100,000
Total depreciation after last five years	$272,727	$327,680	$443,705	$500,000

PICKING UP *clues* from *financial* STATEMENTS

For instance, let's say you want to buy a house. When you approach your bank for a mortgage, what kind of questions will the loan officer ask you? For starters, she'll want to know how much money you make. She'll then ask what your annual expenses are, to see if your salary can cover them. She'll want to know if you have any collateral, or assets to back the loan. And finally, she'll want to know if you can afford your mortgage payments.

The bank does this to determine whether you are financially capable of meeting your obligations. Companies, similarly, analyze their finances to determine their own solvency, to satisfy regulatory requirements, and, most important, to gauge their performance.

When assessing themselves, companies seek the kind of information that the loan officer in our example sought: an accounting of revenues, expenses, assets, liabilities, and liquidity.

To keep track of all these things, they rely on three key financial statements: the income statement, the balance sheet, and the cash flow statement.

Income Statement

The income statement, sometimes called the statement of earnings or the P&L (which stands for profit and loss), is the principal tool businesses use to gauge *profitability*. It demonstrates how well a company has performed over a specific period of time in terms of revenues, expenses, and earnings.

Key Elements of the Income Statement

ACCOUNTING HAS A POINT OF VIEW

A basic concept of accounting states that each company must be treated as an individual entity. Financial statements must be prepared with this in mind—and from the company's point of view.

Sales

The first line in many income statements shows a company's net sales, or revenues. If you've ever wondered why people refer to a company's sales growth as "top-line growth," it's because revenues are typically the top line in most income statements. You'll see a hypothetical income statement for Playtown Toys in the chart "Key Elements of the Income Statement" (on page 58). You'll notice that the company generated $560 million in revenue this year. You'll also notice that the income statement shows you how well the company did last year. This comparative data allows you to calculate that the company's revenues rose 14.3 percent this year.

Two Ways to Read the Financials

Investors and financial managers can assess a company's financial statements in one of two ways:

- *Horizontal analysis.* When investors and financial managers compare a company's performance this year—in terms of assets, liabilities, revenues, and expenses—with its performance in previous years, they are using horizontal analysis. A typical question that arises in horizontal analysis is: How fast are net sales growing from year to year?

- *Vertical analysis.* When investors and financial managers analyze a company's assets, liabilities, revenues, and expenses within a singular financial statement, they are using vertical analysis. A typical question that arises in vertical analysis is: What percentage of this years cost of goods sold does labor represent?

Cost of Goods Sold

The next line in the P&L measures a company's direct costs, or those that are specifically related to the acquisition, production, and distribution of its products. For instance, Playtown Toys' cost of goods sold would include its raw material costs, labor costs, and shipping and warehousing expenses.

You'll notice that this year, Playtown's cost of goods sold rose $50 million, to $350 million. Given its 14.3 percent rise in sales, though, the 16.7 percent rise in cost of goods sold isn't necessarily a problem.

Key Elements of the Income Statement
Playtown Toy Company

For the years ending:	Dec. 27, 1997	Dec. 29, 1996
Net Sales	$560,000,000	$490,000,000
Cost of Goods Sold	(350,000,000)	(300,000,000)
Gross Income	210,000,000	190,000,000
Research & Development	(5,000,000)	(5,000,000)
Selling Costs	(30,000,000)	(30,000,000)
General & Administrative	(80,000,000)	(70,000,000)
Depreciation/Amortization Expense	(6,000,000)	(5,000,000)
Operating Income	89,000,000	80,000,000
Interest Income	2,000,000	2,000,000
Interest Expense	(19,000,000)	(15,000,000)
Income Before Taxes	72,000,000	67,000,000
Income Taxes	(28,000,000)	(25,000,000)
Net Income	$44,000,000	$42,000,000

Gross Income

Once you subtract the cost of goods sold from net sales, you get something called gross income. Don't confuse gross income with total profits, or the bottom line. What you're looking for here is whether the company's gross profits are large enough to cover other costs.

Indirect Costs

To find out if the company generated enough gross profits to cover its other expenses, the income statement begins to subtract out various indirect costs. Indirect costs are expenses that aren't specifically attributable to the acquisition, production, or distribution of products. Included in this list are the cost of bonuses, business travel, and consulting fees. Indirect costs are generally broken down into the following broad categories:

- Research & Development

- Selling Costs

- General & Administrative

- Depreciation and Amortization Expense

Pay close attention to depreciation and amortization expenses. When we discuss the balance sheet later in this chapter, we'll show you how this line item interacts with the balance sheet.

According to its income statement Playtown's indirect costs rose 10 percent, from $110 million last year to $121 million this year.

Operating Income

Once you subtract all the indirect costs from gross income, you get operating income. In our example, Playtown Toys generated operating income of $89 million this year, up 11.3 percent from the previous year. But operating income isn't the bottom line, either. There are still other costs and revenue to consider.

Interest Income

Over the course of a year, companies invest their cash in a variety of vehicles, such as bank accounts, money-market funds, stocks, bonds, or other businesses. But unless the company you're analyzing is a financial institution, this line item tends to be small in most income statements. In Playtown Toys' case, for instance, the company generated just $2 million in interest income, the same amount it earned last year.

Interest Expense

Companies also borrow money, for a variety of reasons. Some do it to finance expansion. Others do it to help pay for day-to-day business activities. (We'll explain exactly why and how companies borrow money in chapter 13.) The income statement also captures this activity. For instance, this year interest expenses cost Playtown Toys $19 million, versus $15 million last year.

Income Before Taxes

Once you add interest income and subtract interest expenses, you learn that Playtown's income before taxes is $72 million, up from $67 million the previous year.

Income Taxes

The income statement now subtracts taxes from Playtown's *income before taxes*. This year, taxes cost Playtown Toys $28 million, leaving it with a *net income* of $44 million, up 5 percent from last year.

Net Income

Net income refers to a company's actual profits, or bottom line. The term "bottom line" comes from the fact that net income is usually the last line on an income statement. Note: Increased revenues don't always guarantee increased profits. In our example, for instance, though Playtown's sales rose 14.3 percent, net income rose only 5 percent. That's why it's always important to consider the "bottom line."

Balance Sheet

While the income statement tells you how well a company has *performed* over a specific period of time covered by the statement, the balance sheet measures a company's overall financial *health* at a given moment in time. Lenders use this information to determine the creditworthiness of a company, but you can use it to gauge a company's overall *risk*.

The balance sheet is divided into three broad categories: assets, liabilities, and shareholder equity as shown on pages 62 and 63. You'll recall in chapter 3 that the basic equation of accounting is that: Assets = Liabilities + Shareholder Equity. You're about to see this play itself out.

Key Elements of a Balance Sheet

Current Assets

The balance sheet begins by assessing a company's current assets. The definition of a current asset is an asset that will be converted into cash in the normal operation of business—generally within a year. If you look at our hypothetical balance sheet (on page 62), the Playtown Toy Co. currently has $194 million in total current assets. Its current assets are broken into the following categories:

- *Cash and cash equivalents.* Cash is a company's most liquid asset. In our example, Playtown Toys has $5 million.

- *Accounts receivable.* While less liquid than cash, companies generally receive payments on these credit accounts within 30 to 60 days. Playtown has $91 million tied up in accounts receivable. That means nearly half of its current assets are tied up in receivables.

BOOK VS. MARKET VALUE

Don't confuse a company's book value with its *market value*. A company's book value refers to a measure of its net worth, or shareholder equity. Its market value is determined by what investors are willing to pay for it. This is commonly done by taking the number of shares of stock a company has outstanding and multiplying that by the market price per share for the stock.

Key Elements of a Balance Sheet
Playtown Toy Company

For the years ending:	Dec. 27, 1997	Dec. 29, 1996
Assets		
Current Assets:		
Cash and Cash Equivalents	$5,000,000	$6,000,000
Accounts Receivable	91,000,000	70,000,000
Inventories	98,000,000	100,000,000
Total Current Assets	194,000,000	176,000,000
Property, Plant & Equipment:		
Land	$ 10,000,000	$8,000,000
Buildings & Improvements	60,000,000	55,000,000
Machinery & Equipment	34,000,000	30,000,000
Less Accumulated Depreciation	(4,000,000)	(3,000,000)
Total Property, Plant & Equipment	100,000,000	90,000,000
Other Assets:		
Intangible Assets	$272,000,000	$180,000,000
Less Amortization	(2,000,000)	(2,000,000)
Total Intangible Assets	270,000,000	178,000,000
Total Assets	$564,000,000	$444,000,000

For the years ending:	Dec. 27, 1997	Dec. 29, 1996

Liabilities and Shareholder Equity

Current Liabilities:

Current Portion of Long-Term Debt	$10,000,000	$10,000,000
Accounts Payable	40,000,000	35,000,000
Accrued Payroll	50,000,000	40,000,000
Total Current Liabilities	100,000,000	85.000.000
Long-Term Debt:	200,000,000	139,000,000
Total Liabilities	$300,000,000	$224,000,000

Shareholder Equity:

Owner's Investment	$100,000,000	$100,000,000
Paid-In Capital	120,000,000	78.000.000
Retained Earnings	44,000,000	42,000,000
Total Shareholder Equity	$264,000,000	$220,000,000
Total Liabilities and Shareholder Equity	$564,000,000	$444,000,000

- *Inventories.* Inventory is considered the least liquid of the current assets. The majority of companies convert inventory into cash in well under a year. If they can't, it's a sure sign that they're in trouble. In our example, Playtown has $98 million, or 51 percent of its total current assets, in inventory.

Property, Plant, and Equipment

In addition to current assets, companies have fixed assets on their books. Fixed assets, as we mentioned in chapter 3, are those that aren't intended to be liquidated in the normal course of business. In general, they tend to be those with long life expectancies—such as buildings or heavy equipment.

If you look at our hypothetical balance sheet, you'll see that Playtown Toys owns $104 million in land, buildings, and machinery.

This does not mean that the company's facilities and equipment are necessarily *worth* that much. This is the *historic cost* of these assets, which, as we noted, is required by GAAP for the purpose of reporting assets on a balance sheet. However, the company has already depreciated $4 million off the value of its buildings and equipment. You can tell by looking at the line item entitled *accumulated depreciation,* just below land, buildings, and equipment. This represents the amount of its assets that have been *written off* the books. When a company does this, it must *expense* that amount to its income statement, under the line item entitled *depreciation and amortization expense.* Here's a perfect example of how the income statement and balance sheet communicate with each other.

Intangible Assets

In addition to property, plant, and equipment, companies carry other *fixed assets* on their books. One such example: intangible assets. Intangibles include such things as patents, copyrights, and goodwill. Like buildings, patents are "of value" to a company. In fact, if you look at Playtown's balance sheet, you'll notice that it has $272 million in intangible assets—nearly three times its stake in property, plant, and equipment. That's because for some companies, patents and copyrights are more valuable than bricks and mortar.

You'll notice that like a building, an intangible asset can be depreciated over time. When an intangible is depreciated, though, it is referred to as amortization. Playtown amortized $2 million off its $272 million worth of intangible assets.

One more thing: If you add the $2 million the company amortized off its intangible assets to the $4 million it depreciated off its property, plant, and equipment, you arrive at $6 million—the amount of money Playtown expensed this year on its income statement under the heading *depreciation/amortization expense.*

Total Assets

According to its balance sheet, the Playtown Toy Co. has $564 million in total assets.

Current Liabilities

Current liabilities are debts and obligations in which payment is due in a year or less. In our example, Playtown Toys has $100 million in current liabilities. They are broken down into the following categories:

- *Current portion of long-term debt.* This represents that portion of interest—and perhaps principal—due on the company's long-term debt within the next 12 months. If you glance over at Playtown's balance sheet, you'll see that the company owes $10 million within the next year. Its total long-term debt, though, stands at $200 million.

- *Accounts payable.* This represents money owed to suppliers, as explained in chapter 3. Playtown owes $40 million in accounts payable.

- *Accrued payroll.* This represents the money the company owes within the next year in payroll expenses. For Playtown, that figure comes to $50 million.

Long-Term Debt

Long-term debt represents loans and other sources of long-term financing the company is obligated to repay beyond the next 12 months. Playtown currently owes $200 million in long-term debt.

Total Liabilities

You can add up a company's current liabilities and its long-term debt to find out what its total liabilities are. Playtowns's total liabilities are $300 million.

Shareholder Equity

Now, we come to the shareholder equity component of the balance sheet. You'll recall that shareholder equity is another term for net worth. While it can be measured in the equation, *assets – liabilities = net worth*, there is another, equally simple way companies derive this figure: by calculating the total investments made in the firm.

The formula is quite simple: Take the original investment the owners of a company made in the firm; add all other capital invested in the company since that time; and finally, add in retained earnings. Retained earnings simply represent the net income a company generated over the course of a year minus that portion it chose to distribute to its investors, in the form of dividends. That simple formula—*owners original investment + paid-in capital + retained earnings* = gives us total shareholder equity. Let's see how this plays itself out in Playtown's case.

First, we know that Playtown's owners' original investment amounted to $100 million. Second, we know that the amount of paid-in capital at the end of this year was $120 million.

	Dec. 27, 1997	Dec. 29, 1996
Owner's Investment	$100,000,000	$100,000,000
Paid-In Capital	120,000,000	78,000,000

That gives us two parts of this three-part equation: $100 million (owners' investment) + $120 million (paid-in capital) + ? = shareholder equity.

To figure out the missing piece—retained earnings—all we need to know is how much the company earned in net income this year and how much it paid out in dividends. Well, Playtown's income statement shows that it earned $44 million at the end of this year. And Playtown did not pay out any dividends this year. That means all $44 million in net income was reinvested in the company in the form of *retained earnings*. So, we add $100 million (owners' investment) to $120 million (paid-in capital) and to $44 million (retained earnings) and we conclude that Playtown's shareholder equity is $264 million.

All of this is played out in a fourth financial statement—Playtown's Reconciliation of Net Worth Statement. This simple statement reflects what we just described above.

The beginning balance refers to the total net worth the company enjoyed at the beginning of the year. This amounts to the total of money invested in the company as of the end of last year. We can figure this out by looking at Playtown's shareholder equity line item in its balance sheet last year. By doing so, we find out that the company's net worth last year was $220 million. Next, we add in the company's profits—$44 million. Finally, we subtract out dividends paid. Once again, Playtown did not distribute dividends to its investors this year. By adding $220 million with $44 million, we come out with $264 million.

Playtown Toy Company
Reconciliation of Net Worth Statement

		Dec. 27, 1997
Beginning Balance		$220,000,000
Net Income	$44,000,000	
Less Dividends	(0)	
Retained Earnings		44,000,000
End Balance		$264,000,000

Similarly, we can arrive at that same figure by taking the company's assets—$564 million— and subtracting out its liabilities, or $300 million.

As you can see, there is an elegance to finance.

The Annual Report

Publicly traded companies are required by SEC regulations to produce an *annual report* and to distribute it to shareholders every year. Privately held companies may or may not choose to produce such a document. If you've ever invested in a stock, you've probably seen what these reports look like. Annual reports include:

- *Basic corporate information*, including the name and address of the company; the names and addresses of each subsidiary; the names and addresses of transfer agents and the registrar of the company; the names of the company's executives; and the names of the company's board of directors.

- *Letter to shareholder*. The chairman of the board or the CEO usually includes a one-page letter focusing on key developments and events that affected the company's performance—and stock price—during the past year.

- *Financial highlights*. The company will generally point out several positive achievements the company made during the year. This may or may not include charts and graphs showing stock price fluctuations (if positive) and sales and earnings figures (once again, if positive).

- *Review of operations*. Here, the company discusses specific achievements, product releases, acquisitions, and any other major events that took place over the course of the year.

- *Financial statements*. This includes a balance sheet, income statement, statement of cash flows, and statement of retained earnings.

(continued)

- *Footnotes to the financial statements.* Any special accounting practices, such as one-time asset write-offs, must be disclosed in these footnotes.

- *Management discussion.* The SEC requires management to address specific issues in their financial statements.

The Cash Flow Statement

The income statement tells you how much profit your company has generated over a specific period of time. And the balance sheet tells you what its net worth is at a given moment in time. But there's a hitch: Most businesses rely on *accrual basis accounting.* Under accrual accounting, you'll recall, a company books its sales and expenses *before* it receives or makes payment for those transactions. So, even though sales may outpace expenses on the income statement and assets may outpace liabilities on the balance sheet, a company may have less cash flowing in than is flowing out of its accounts during a specific period of time. And this could spell trouble. That's one reason why companies turn to a third major financial statement, called the cash flow statement.

Cash flow statements record the following:

1. Cash inflow and outflow from operations

2. Cash inflow and outflow from investing

3. Cash inflow and outflow from financing

The cash flow statement works under a simple set of premises:

Key Elements of a Cash Flow Statement
Playtown Toy Company

For the year ending:	Dec. 27, 1997
Cash and Cash Equivalents, Beginning of Year	$6,000,000
Cash flow from operations:	
Net Income	2,000,000
Accounts Receivable	(21,000,000)
Inventories	2,000,000
Accounts Payable	5,000,000
Accumulated Depreciation/Amortization	1,000,000
Accrued Payroll	10,000,000
Cash flow from investing:	
Property, Plant & Equipment	(11,000,000)
Intangible Assets	(92,000,000)
Cash flow from financing:	
Current Portion of Long-Term Debt	0
Long-Term Debt	61,000,000
Dividend Payment	0
Owners' Investment + Capital	42,000,000
New Total: Cash and Cash Equivalents, End of Year	$5,000,000

- Cash flows out of a company when there is *an increase in an asset.*

- Cash flows into a company when there is *a decrease in an asset.*

- Cash flows into a company when there is *an increase in a liability.*

- Cash flows out of a company when there is *a decrease in a liability.*

- Cash flows out of a company when there is *a decrease in net worth.*

- Cash flows into a company when there is *an increase in net worth.*

Notice that we use the term *increase* and *decrease.* When assembling a cash flow statement, what's important is the change in assets and liabilities from one period to another—not the actual dollar figures. For instance, we know that inventory is an asset. Let's say that your company has $10 million of inventory on its balance sheet this year, compared with $3 million last year. We would record that as a $7 million *outflow* of cash on the cash flow statement ($10 million minus $3 million). That's because an increase in assets is considered a *decrease* in cash. Conceptually, you can understand why. To increase its inventory by $7 million, your company would have had to spend $7 million in cash.

Similarly, let's assume your company has increased its short-term debt from $7 million last year to $20 million this year. The $13 million increase in debt—a liability— would be noted in the cash flow statement as a $13 million *inflow* of cash. This, too, makes sense. When your company obtains financing, it receives capital to inject into its business.

Now, let's take a look at what Playtown Toys' cash flow statement would look like. The "Key Elements of a Cash Flow Statement" chart on page 70 was compiled using information from Playtown's balance sheet and income statement.

Cash Flow from Operations

The sign of a healthy company is one that has enough cash flowing into its accounts to offset cash flowing out. In fact, many investors look to rising cash flow as a criterion for

buying a company's stock. In terms of gauging a company's cash flow, investors start off by studying a company's *cash flow from operations.* Right off the bat, you'll notice that under Net Income, Playtown's cash flow statement lists $2 million. You may be asking yourself: "How can that be? I thought Playtown earned $44 million last year?" It did. But remember that cash flow statements record the *change in cash.* That means the company had to consider how its net income changed from the beginning of the year to the end. Well, its income statement showed that it earned $44 million versus $42 million last year. That's a $2 million increase in net worth. So we treat this as a source of cash.

Cash flow from operations:

Net Income	$2,000,000
Assets	
Accounts Receivable	(21,000,000)
Inventories	2,000,000
Liabilities	
Accounts Payable	5,000,000
Accumulated Depreciation/Amortization	1,000,000
Accrued Payroll	10,000,000
Cash flow from operations	$(1,000,000)

Playtown's accounts receivable position also changed. This year, the company had $91 million in receivables, versus $70 million last year. That's a $21 million increase. But since an *increase in an asset* is considered a use of cash, we actually subtract it from our cash flow. Hence, the parentheses surrounding that line item.

Inventories are another part of a company's normal operations. But in Playtown's cash, inventory actually fell $2 million from last year to this year, according to its balance sheet. Since inventories are an asset and a decrease in an asset is considered a source of cash, we *add* that to our cash flow.

Now, we get to the company's liabilities. Accounts payable grew $5 million, from $35 million last year to $40 million this year. We consider this a source of cash. Depreciation and amortization increased $1 million from last year to this year. That's another source of cash. Finally, accrued payroll jumped from $40 million last year to $50 million this year. That's a $10 million source of cash. Grand total: Playtown had a net $1 million outflow of cash from operations.

Cash Flow from Investing

Since fixed assets are not intended to be converted to cash in the normal course of business, companies that acquire these assets are making an investment in themselves. That's why the two major categories listed in Playtown's cash flow statement under investing are property, plant, and equipment and its intangible assets.

Why did Playtown record an $11 million outflow of cash from property, plant, and equipment? Simple. Prior to depreciation (since we already accounted for it in our cash flow statement under operations), Playtown's property, plant, and equipment totaled $104 million. That's $11 million more than last year. Since an increase in an asset is a use of cash, Playtown records this as an $11 million outflow.

The same is true for its intangible assets. This year (subtracting out amortization), Playtown's intangible assets are listed at $272 million. Last year, they were at $180 million. That's a $92 million use of cash. Grand total: a $103 million use of cash.

Cash flow from investing:	
Property, Plant & Equipment	$(11,000,000)
Intangible Assets	(92,000,000)
Cash flow from investing	(103,000,000)

Cash flow from financing:

Current Portion of Long-Term Debt	$0
Long-Term Debt	61,000,000
Dividend Payment	0
Owners' Investment + Capital	42,000,000
Cash flow from financing	$103,000,000

Cash Flow from Financing

Finally, we come to the final category—the change in Playtown's cash position due to financing. Financing comes in many forms. For instance, some companies may have a number of separate short-term, intermediate-term, and long-term debts. All forms of debt represent a liability. So we would treat an increase in debt as a source of cash, and a decrease in debt as a use of cash (this makes sense, since we require cash to pay down debt).

If you look at the first line item under financing—the current portion of long-term debt—you'll notice that Playtown lists $0. That doesn't mean that Playtown doesn't owe money in the next 12 months to cover portions of its long-term debt. Rather, the $0 simply reflects the fact that the company owes no more (or less) than it did the previous year.

Playtown's long-term debt picture, however, has changed, if you recall from its balance sheet. Playtown indicated in its balance sheet that it now owes $200 million in long-term debt, versus $139 million the previous year. That's an increase of $61 million—a source of cash.

Now we come to those portions of financing that relate to Playtown's net worth. You'll recall from the company's Net Worth Reconciliation Statement that all of its earnings were reinvested into the company. That means the company paid out $0 in dividends, just as it did the previous year. That means its dividend situation hasn't changed. As for owner's investment + capital, this refers to the change in situation in terms of both these categories. Last year, owners' investment and capital amounted to $178 million. This year, it stood at $220 million, reflecting the $42 million in profits from last year reinvested in the company. That's why Playtown's cash flow statement indicates a $42 million use of cash here.

Now comes the final tally. We know that Playtown *used* $1 million in cash for operations and $103 million for investing. At the same time, it saw an inflow of $103 million in cash from financing. That suggests $1 million greater outflow than inflow. Now, we add that negative $1 million in cash to the company's beginning cash balance—$6 million, derived from its year-end balance on last year's balance sheet—and we come up with a final tally of $5 million in cash. Now, take a look at the company's balance sheet. Notice that its cash and cash equivalents stood at $5 million at the end of this year. See how that works?

USING
key
financial
RATIOS

Sometimes the income statement, balance sheet, and statement of cash flows aren't enough to provide a clear picture of a company's finances.

For instance, in our hypothetical example, Playtown Toys earned $44 million this year, according to its income statement. How can you tell if that's good? One way is to compare the company's performance with competing toy companies. But what if there are no toy companies Playtown's size? Would it be fair to compare the earnings of a company with $560 million in sales versus that of a company that generates $2 billion in sales?

Of course not. This is why we turn to financial ratios for help.

Comparing Apples with Apples Using Financial Ratios

Financial ratios are tools—based on information from income statements and balance sheets—used to gauge a company's *relative* performance. Like financial statements, they gauge profitability, liquidity, and risk.

By measuring performance in percentage terms—rather than raw numbers—these ratios allow us to compare our company's performance against industry peers and to set reasonable performance goals. For instance, let's say your best friend wanted to open a restaurant. Not having any experience in the business, he asks you what you think is a reasonable profit he should expect. Without ratios, you couldn't even begin to guess. Would $500,000 be more reasonable than $1,000,000? How can you tell without knowing how big his restaurant would be and how much it would generate in sales? With ratios, though, you can just look it up—there are at least three good sources for finding this information. Ratio analysis, for instance, tells us that recently the typical restaurant's net profit margin was 3.3 percent. So your friend will know that he ought to expect profit margins of roughly that much. By comparing its ratios over time versus those of competitors, your company can spot its long-term financial performance trends.

TO FIND INDUSTRY AVERAGES...

...you can contact an industry association. Or, you can look up financial ratios in one of three published books: *Annual Statement Studies* (Robert Morris Associates, 1997); *Industry Norms and Key Business Ratios* (Dun & Bradstreet, 1996–1997); and the *Almanac of Business and Industrial Ratios* (Prentice-Hall, 1997).

Four Quick Back-of-the-Envelope Calculations to Measure Profitability

Gross Margin

To calculate: *Gross Income/Net Sales = Gross Margin*

Purpose: This ratio describes the profit margin your company enjoys on the goods it sells, after

Some Basic
Industry Averages

Industry	Gross Margin	Net Margin	ROA	Current Ratio	Quick Ratio	DSO
Retail	33.5	3.2	4.8	3.6	0.8	8.0
Furniture	34.6	3.8	6.5	2.4	0.9	22.3
Hardware	33.5	2.9	4.6	3.2	0.8	18.8
Restaurant	52.6	3.3	7.0	1.1	0.6	4.8
Newspapers	52.6	5.2	7.4	1.8	1.3	39.1
Telecomm.	39.7	13.4	6.7	1.9	1.2	56.9
Entertainment	53.4	8.3	9.2	2.6	1.5	28.8
Software	60.2	5.1	8.6	2.1	1.6	70.0
Advertising	35.2	5.4	7.9	1.4	1.3	54.4

direct costs have been subtracted out. Direct costs, you'll remember, are expenses companies incur buying, producing, and distributing their products.

Though a somewhat crude gauge of overall profits, gross margins tell companies how well they are controlling direct costs.

For instance, in our hypothetical example from chapter 5, Playtown's gross margin this year was 37.5 percent ($210 million/$560 million). That means for every $1 the company generated in sales, it pocketed 37.5 cents in gross profits.

That's 3.8 cents worse than the typical toy company and 1.3 cents worse than its performance last year.

Operating Margin

To calculate: *Operating Income/Net Sales = Operating Profit Margin*

Purpose: Operating margins let you know how well companies are managing their *indirect costs,* such as overhead. If you find that your company's gross margins are rising while its operating margins are falling, you'll know immediately that the company is having difficulty controlling indirect costs.

In our example, Playtown saw its operating margin fall from 16.3 percent last year to 15.9 percent this year ($89,000,000/$560,000,000). At the same time, its gross margin fell from 38.8 percent last year to 37.5 percent this year.

Net Margin

To calculate: *Net Income/Net Sales = Net Margin*

Purpose: If you want to find out how much *profit* a company generates, you turn to its net income figure. If you want to find out how *profitable* a company is, you look at its net margin.

In our example, Playtown saw its net margin fall slightly from 8.6 percent in 1996 to 7.9 percent in 1997 ($44,000,000/$560,000,000). This means that for every $1 in sales it generated, Playtown pocketed 7.9 cents. We can then observe, through industry ratio averages, that its peers managed to pocket only 4.1 cents for every $1 in sales.

Return on Investment (ROI)

Thus far, we've discussed gross margin, operating margin, and net margin. They measure a company's profitability *based on sales, as shown in the income statement.* ROI ratios measure a company's profitability a different way—relative to investments and/or assets.

The two most common ways to measure ROI are *return on equity* and *return on assets.*

Return on Equity (ROE)

To calculate: *Net Income/Shareholder Equity = ROE*

Purpose: ROE lets us know whether a company is worthwhile as an investment, based on its level of profitability. For instance, if a company generates an ROE of 25 percent, it means an investment in that firm will yield a 25 percent return.

In our example, Playtown's ROE was 16.7 percent ($44,000,000/$264,000,000), down slightly from 19.1 percent the previous year. That's roughly in line with the typical large company in America, which returned about 18 percent on shareholder equity in 1997.

If you're an investor, this tells you that putting your money in this company is worthwhile. If you're management, this tells you that a decent way to maximize shareholder equity is to invest more of the company's earnings back into the business.

Return on Assets (ROA)

To calculate: *Net Income/Total Assets = ROA*

Purpose: Since ROA measures a company's profits against its assets, you can use ROA analysis to compare the profitability of companies of various sizes against one another.

In our example, Playtown Toys enjoyed an ROA of 7.8 percent based on its $564 million in total assets ($44,000,000/$564,000,000). That's slightly worse than the 9.5 percent it returned on assets last year, but slightly better than the industry average of 7 percent.

But let's take this example one step further. Recall that we told you in chapter 3 that Playtown has two divisions: Electronic Games and Traditional Toys. Let's assume that the Electronic Games division generated 60 percent of the company's income, or $26.4 million, while controlling only 40 percent of the company's assets, or $225.6 million. That means that the Electronic Games division enjoys an ROA of 11.7 percent compared with just 5.2 percent ($17.6 million/$338.4 million) for the Traditional Toys unit.

Are Companies More Profitable Today?

That's certainly the impression you'd get if all you looked at was *return on equity*.

A decade ago, the typical large company's ROE was about 10 percent. Today, it's closer to 18 percent. It's not that companies make more profits. It's the fact that companies have written off a record amount of assets during the 1990s as a result of restructurings.

How do asset write-offs impact ROE? Since shareholder equity is the denominator in the ROE equation *(Net Income/Shareholder Equity)*, the smaller your company's shareholder equity is, the greater its ROE will be. Asset write-offs, by definition, reduce shareholder equity, since, as we mentioned in chapter 3, shareholder equity equals assets minus liabilities. (Note: Assets written off must be charged against earnings in the year they were written off. So technically, write-offs also affect the numerator of this equation—net income. However, many investors overlook the impact of so-called one-time charges against profits because they are considered extraordinary events.)

Tip: If you're an investor scanning the market for the most profitable companies, you can still rely on ROE. Just make sure you stick with companies with low debt that have not taken many write-offs recently. And make sure that their financials are in order.

If management decides to invest additional money into the company, ratio analysis should tell it that more of that money ought to go to Electronic Games, since $1 of assets invested in this division yields a greater profit than $1 invested in Traditional Toys.

Two Shortcuts to Measure Liquidity

Current Ratio

To calculate: *Current Assets/Current Liabilities = Current Ratio*

Purpose: The current ratio lets you know if a company has at least enough liquid assets to cover its short-term obligations—those that will come due in the next one month to one year. A high current ratio indicates that a company can *probably* meets its debts. This ratio does not, however, tell you if it can *actually* do so. There's always the possibility that your company might not be able to convert all of its current assets into cash in the normal operation of business as fast as it would like.

Investors tend to favor companies with a current ratio of at least 2:1. Our hypothetical company's current ratio is 1.94 to 1, based on current liabilities of $100 million and current assets of $194 million ($194,000,000/$100,000,000=1.94).

Quick Ratio

To calculate: *(Current Assets – Inventory)/Current Liabilities = Quick Ratio*

Purpose: This ratio tells you what the current ratio does not. By subtracting out inventories from current assets, the quick ratio tells you if a company can *actually* cover its short-term obligations with its liquid assets.

This is why some refer to this as the *acid test.* Investors tend to favor companies with a quick ratio of at least 1:1. Obviously, the higher the ratio, the safer the company is.

KEY PROFITABILITY RATIOS

- Gross Margin
- Operating Margin
- Net Margin
- Return on Equity
- Return on Assets

KEY LIQUIDITY RATIOS

- Current Ratio

- Quick Ratio

KEY RISK RATIOS

- Debt Ratio

- Debt-to-Equity Ratio

KEY MANAGEMENT RATIOS

- Inventory Turnover

- Days Sales Outstanding

In our example, Playtown has a quick ratio of 0.96 to 1, based on current assets of $194 million, inventories of $98 million, and current liabilities of $100 million [(194,000,000–$98,000,000)/ $100,000,000 = .96].

Two Quick Ways to Measure Risk

Debt Ratio

To calculate: *Total Liabilities/Total Assets = Debt Ratio*

Purpose: Since Assets – Liabilities = Net Worth, a debt ratio of greater than 1 says that the company is entering into *negative net worth territory*. In our example, Playtown's debt ratio is just 0.532 percent, based on total liabilities of $300 million and total assets of $564 million.

Debt-to-Equity Ratio

To calculate: *Total Liabilities/Shareholder Equity = Debt-to-Equity Ratio*

Purpose: As a company's *total liabilities* exceed its net worth, it risks the ability to obtain financing. In our example, Playtown's debt-to-equity ratio is 114 percent. That's not too good. But, investors rely on another, similar measure: long-term debt-to-capital. Here, you divide long-term debt by shareholder equity added to long-term

debt. Playtown's long-term debt-to-capital ratio is 43.1 percent. That's a bit more reassuring. In 1997, the typical large company had a long-term debt-to-capital ratio of around 42 percent.

Two Ways to Tell If Management Is Doing Its Job

Inventory Turnover

To calculate: *Cost of Goods Sold/Inventory = Inventory Turnover*

Purpose: The speed with which a company can move its inventory indicates how popular its merchandise is; how effective its sales force is; and how well managed its assets are. Rising inventory turnover is a sign of a healthy company. Consider $34 billion Intel, the world's leading maker of microprocessing chips for personal computers. Intel increased the number of times its inventory turns over in a year from 3.9 in 1995 to seven times just two years later. Based on net sales of $560 million and inventory of $98 million, Playtown's inventory turnover ratio is 3.6.

A related ratio that some companies use is called the *age of inventory* ratio. This one takes the inventory turnover rate and divides it *into* 365 days. For Playtown, we would take its turnover of 3.6 and divide that into 365. This means that the company's inventory is generally held for 101 days before sale.

RATIO SMOKE AND MIRRORS

You can boost your *quick* or *current* ratios by taking on more long-term debt. The proceeds can be temporarily converted into cash equivalents, which is a current asset. However, the portion of that long-term debt due to be paid in the next 12 months will count toward *current liabilities.*

LESS DEBT

The typical American company in 1997 had a long-term debt-to-capital ratio of about 42 percent. That represents a major improvement. In 1995, the average ratio stood at 58 percent; in 1991, it was a whopping 69 percent.

ONCE A MONTH

Companies in highly cyclical industries must analyze financial ratios at least *once a month.* Those that don't, risk comparing their performance in traditionally weak months with their performance during high volume periods.

Days Sales Outstanding (DSO)

To calculate: *Accounts Receivable/(Net Sales ÷ 365) = DSO*

Purpose: Managers who want to know how quickly their customers are paying their bills rely on the DSO. A rising DSO ratio—which means a slowdown in repayments—signals potential pressure on a company's cash flow. For instance, Playtown's accounts receivable stand at $91 million. Its sales per day ($560,000,000/365) are $1,534,250. That means its DSO is 59.3 days. That's slightly more than the 52.2 days it took its customers to pay their bills last year.

On the other side of the ledger, there is a *days payable* ratio, which shows how long it takes a company to pay its vendors. It is calculated by taking your company's accounts payable, and dividing that by the cost of goods sold per day [Accounts Payable/(Cost of Goods Sold/365)]. This ratio is harder to analyze, though, since most companies like to wait as long as possible to pay their own bills. Why give up your cash until you absolutely have to? We'll explain the value of faster collection and slower payments in chapter 9, when we discuss cash management. In the meantime, we'll show you how companies use these financial ratios—and ratio analysis—to set future expectations for their performance in the following chapter, where we discuss budgets.

UNDERSTANDING
how
budgets
WORK

The principal tool in *planning* is called a budget. Most of you know what a budget is. You probably put one together for your household expenses to figure out, based on what you make, how much you can afford to spend next year.

Businesses rely on budgets, too—for much the same reason.

What Is a Budget?

"A budget is a company's blueprint." You'll hear this phrase often. And it's true. A budget maps out a company's expectations and goals for the coming year. For our discussion, though, think of a budget as a piece of paper—or actually several pieces of paper. On these pieces of paper, companies record their:

- *Past performance, in terms of sales, expenses, earnings, and cash flow.* This information, found in financial statements, financial ratios, and managerial reports, gives companies the context to begin planning for the coming year.

- *Future projections for sales, expenses, earnings, and cash flow.* Based on past performance—in addition to current economic conditions and trends—companies will project next year's sales, expenses, earnings, and cash flow. In fact, when companies establish their budgets, they are in essence approximating what their income statement, balance sheet, and cash flow statements will look like next year. For instance, take a look at our example "Budget for Jim's Sporting Goods" on page 89, which shows a portion of the budget for Jim's Sporting Goods, a company that makes basketballs. You'll notice that the portion of the document shown here looks remarkably similar to a P&L—breaking out sales, direct costs, gross profit, indirect costs, and operating income. The only difference is that next year's figures are based on educated guesses, not actual performance.

That's what we put into our budgets. Here's what we get out of them:

- *Budgets tell us what we'll need to do to break even.* For instance, budgets will show how many widgets a company will need to sell, given its cost structure, to make a profit. In addition, they tell us how many widgets that company must sell to achieve a *desired level of profits.* We'll explain how companies do this in a moment.

- *Budgets remind us how we should allocate our resources.* Like blueprints, budgets remind us what we'll need to set aside—for manufacturing, engineering, marketing, and other purposes—to carry out our business plan.

- *Budgets make sure that everyone is on the same page.* Should there be any confusion about the assumptions, projections, and goals the firm has made, we can turn to the budget to settle disputes.

Budget for Jim's Sporting Goods

	1997	1998 (est.)	Percent Increase
Basketballs Sold	500,000	700,000	40 percent
Total Sales	$5,000,000	$7,000,000	40 percent
Direct Costs:			
Raw Materials	(1,000,000)	(1,800,000)	80 percent
Labor	(1,000,000)	(1,200,000)	20 percent
Total	(2,000,000)	(3,000,000)	50 percent
Gross Profit	$3,000,000	$4,000,000	33 percent
Indirect Costs:			
General & Administrative*	(1,000,000)	(1,000,000)	0 percent
Selling Costs	(500,000)	(500,000)	0 percent
Research & Development	(500,000)	(500,000)	0 percent
Total	(2,000,000)	(2,000,000)	0 percent
Operating Income	$1,000,000	$2,000,000	100 percent

*(includes rent and depreciation)

THE RULE OF THREE

A budget is a collection of predictions. Just because a budget says that a department's revenue and expenses will balance does not mean that they will. So as the year wears on, companies may require some departments to trim costs to make up for bad revenue or expense predictions.

The *Rule of Three* is simply a method to help companies prepare for such a contingency. This rule of budgeting says that a company—or its individual departments—ought to divide itself into three parts: one part that is considered essential, another part that is desirable, and a third part that is dispensable. This way, if a division must pare itself down quickly, so as not to run a deficit, it will already know which units to cut.

- Budgets reinforce our priorities by writing them down on paper. You should be able to glance at a budget and tell, based on the allocation of resources, which products or divisions the company focuses its attention on in the coming year. For instance, knowing that the marketing budget for product A will be three times as large as the budget for product B is an obvious clue that the company is emphasizing product A's sales.

The Various Types of Budgets

A company does not have just one budget. It actually maintains several mini-budgets. They include:

- Sales budgets

- Expense budgets

- Cash budgets

- Capital budgets

Information from these smaller budgets is rolled into a *master budget*. The master budget represents a company's projected P&L statement, balance sheet, and statement of cash flows.

Sales Budgets

Sales budgets indicate projected sales of products, in terms of both *dollars* and *unit sales*. Among all the different types of budgets a company puts together, the sales budget is the most important. That's because every other decision the company makes—in terms of its expenses and long-term investment choices—is predicated on the accuracy and legitimacy of its sales forecasts.

For instance, a large percentage of a company's costs are *variable* costs. That means these expenses—such as raw materials—are predicated on the amount of business the company generates. Jim's Sporting Goods can't estimate the amount of money it'll need to spend for rubber and other raw materials until it knows how many basketballs it plans to make. And it won't know how many basketballs it needs to make until it comes up with a forecast for how many basketballs it thinks it can sell. Thus, the accuracy of Jim's expense forecasts is predicated on the accuracy of its sales budget.

Generally, when a company establishes a sales budget, it breaks information out on a monthly or quarterly basis. You can see an example of this on page 92 in the "Monthly Basketball Sales" chart.

Expense Budgets

Companies assemble several different *expense budgets.* The most important among these is the *cost of goods sold,* or *inventory* budget. If you'll recall, the cost of goods sold includes all those expenses tied to the production and distribution of products, such as raw materials, storage, and labor costs. The projections made on the cost of goods sold budget will be subtracted from projections in the sales budget to determine projected gross profits for the coming year.

PARETO'S LAW

Otherwise known as the 80/20 rule, *Pareto's Law* states that often, 80 percent of a company's output is derived from 20 percent of its input.

Pareto's Law tells companies that they ought to concentrate their efforts on the 20 percent of their operations that generate 80 percent of their production.

Jim's Sporting Goods
Monthly Basketball Sales

	1997 Units Sold	1998 Budget	Percent Change	1997 $ Sales	1998 $ Budget	Percent Change
January	22,000	$27,000	22.7	$220,000	$270,000	22.7
February	19,000	26,000	36.8	190,000	260,000	36.8
March	18,000	27,000	50.0	180,000	270,000	50.0
1st Quarter **Total**	59,000	80,000	35.6	590,000	800,000	35.6
April	30,000	32,000	6.7	300,000	320,000	6.7
May	31,000	38,000	22.6	310,000	380,000	22.6
June	40,000	41,000	2.5	400,000	410,000	2.5
2nd Quarter **Total**	101,000	111,000	9.9	1,010,000	1,110,000	9.9
July	38,000	42,000	10.5	380,000	420,000	10.5
August	41,000	42,000	2.4	410,000	420,000	2.4
September	40,000	50,000	25.0	400,000	500,000	25.0
3rd Quarter **Total**	119,000	134,000	12.6	1,190,000	1,340,000	12.6
October	64,000	75,000	17.2	640,000	750,000	17.2
November	69,000	100,000	44.9	690,000	1,000,000	44.9
December	88,000	200,000	127.3	880,000	2,000,000	127.3
4th Quarter **Total**	221,000	375,000	69.7	2,210,000	3,750,000	69.7
Annual **Total**	500,000	$700,000	40.0	$5,000,000	$7,000,000	40.0

To plan for indirect costs, businesses also establish separate expense budgets that focus on *general & administrative, selling, and research & development costs.* The G&A budget, for instance, would plan for next year's insurance costs, interest expenses, rent, depreciation, support-staff salaries, payroll taxes, property taxes, and licenses and fees. The selling cost budget projects advertising and commission fees. And the research & development budget projects R&D expenses for the coming year.

Cash Budget

The cash budget is used to project whether the company will have enough cash flowing into its accounts on a weekly or monthly or quarterly basis to cover payments that must be made during those weeks, months, and quarters. If you look at the example labeled "Cash Budget" on the next page, you can see some of the considerations that go into a cash budget.

Cash budgets involve an added degree of complexity. While sales and expense budgets require companies to project how much money will be flowing in and out, the cash budget requires projections on when that money will flow into and out of the company's accounts. That's an outgrowth of the accrual basis of accounting. Cash budgets should reflect any changes a company has made or plans to make in its cash and credit policies (see chapters 9 and 10). In addition, cash budgets should anticipate one-time expenditures, such as the planned purchase of a major piece of equipment.

Master Budget

Information derived from the various budgets is fed into a mega-blueprint known as the *master budget.* The master budget should contain enough information to build projected financial statements for the coming year. The master budget is a so-called *static budget,* which means it is prepared at the beginning of a time period and remains unchanged until the end of that time period. Obviously, budget projections are only educated guesses. So at the end of a specified period of time, actual sales and expenses are recorded, and discrepancies between them and the budgeted numbers are noted. Any discrepancy between actual and budgeted numbers is called a *variance.*

Jim's Sporting Goods
Cash Budget

	March	April	May
Cash at beginning of month	$500,000	$645,000	$330,000
Cash flow in from:			
Current Sales	200,000	175,000	250,000
Prior Sales	350,000	325,000	375,000
Total Cash	1,050,000	1,145,000	955,000
Cash flow out for:			
Cost of Goods Sold	(200,000)	(215,000)	(225,000)
G&A Expenses	(125,000)	(110,000)	(115,000)
Selling Costs	(55,000)	(50,000)	(60,000)
R&D Costs	(25,000)	(90,000)	(75,000)
Taxes	(0)	(350,000)	(0)
Total Payments	(405,000)	(815,000)	(475,000)
Cash at end of month	$645,000	$330,000	$480,000

Variances

As the year wears on, companies periodically check to see how their actual sales and expenses compare to their budgeted projections. The difference between the projection and the actual numbers is called the *variance*. For instance:

Sales Budget for Jim's Sporting Goods

	Units Sold This Year	Units Sold Budget	Variance Units	Total $ This Year	Total $ Budget	Total $ Variance
Footballs	145,567	167,000	(21,433)	$2,183,505	$2,505,000	($321,495)
Baseballs	1,894,087	1,750,000	144,087	7,576,348	7,000,000	576,348
Basketballs	234,090	250,000	(15,910)	2,809,080	3,000,000	(190,920)

Variances can tell a company a lot about its performance. For instance, they can reveal those departments or products that performed below expectations. And they can highlight those that overperformed. (Analyzing variances is tricky though. An exceedingly high variance between projected and actual sales of basketballs for Jim's Sporting Goods, for instance, could indicate that the company underperformed during the year. Or it could simply be a reflection of the poor sales projection methods of the budgeting department.)

Since there's no way to tell if a company's projected sales will actually materialize, companies often construct a second type of budget to work in conjunction with the master budget. These so-called *flexible budgets* provide full projections for expenses depending on a company's sales.

For instance, let's say Jim's sells 1 million basketballs next year, not the 700,000 it had budgeted. What will that do to its cost structure? You can find out by looking at the company's flexible budget, in the example "Flexible Budget" on page 97.

STATIC BUDGETS VS. FLEXIBLE BUDGETS

A *static budget* is used to determine projections based on a specific assumption. For instance, a computer maker may project sales of 10,000 PCs in the coming year. Under a static budget, that computer maker will project its revenues, cost of goods sold, and other expenses based on that assumption.

A *flexible,* or *dynamic budget* on the other hand, will make a number of different projections just in case the original assumption turns out to be wrong.

Capital Budget

The capital budget projects the costs and income associated with a company's long-term projects and fixed assets. These assets include equipment and facilities that have been purchased for:

- *Expansion.* This includes expansion into new regions and expansion through the development and manufacture of new products. For instance, if Jim's Sporting Goods wants to expand into Latin America, it may need to build a distribution center there. If Jim's decided to manufacture hockey pucks in addition to its basketballs, baseballs, and soccer balls, it would need to purchase the equipment to make pucks.

- *Replacement.* On occasion, a company's existing facilities and equipment need to be replaced due to age and condition.

- *Improvement.* On occasion, a company's existing facilities and equipment need to be replaced of upgraded due to improvements in technology, which offer greater efficiency.

- *Miscellaneous purposes.* Sometimes, companies invest in fixed assets for convenience or aesthetics. One example might be the large-scale remodeling of offices. Another would be the acquisition of a vehicle fleet for company executives.

Jim's Sporting Goods
Flexible Budget

Basketballs Sold	500,000	700,000	1,000,000
Revenue	$5,000,000	$7,000,000	$10,000,000
Variable Costs:			
Raw Materials	(1,000,000)	(1,800,000)	(2,500,000)
Labor	(1,000,000)	(1,200,000)	(1,500,000)
Total Fixed Costs	(2,000,000)	(2,000,000)	(2,000,000)
Operating Income	$1,000,000	$2,000,000	$4,000,000

Capital Budgeting

Regardless of why your company enters into a long-term project or asset—be it expansion, replacement, improvement, or miscellaneous purposes—it will need to assess which long-term projects are worth entering into and which are not. Obviously, this decision must be based on an analysis of the long-term project's costs and benefits, referred to as capital budgeting.

To determine which projects are worth entering into—and therefore which projects belong in a capital budget—your company relies on one of the following methods:

- *Payback analysis.* This is the simplest method. Payback analysis asks the question: "If the company invests its money in this long-term project, how long will it take to recover that sum?" To figure this out, companies project the cash flow that the project will generate if entered into; add up each year's total cash inflow for that project; and determine how many years will pass before the original investment is recovered.

For instance, let's say you work for a newspaper company that is deciding whether to invest in a printing press. This press, which costs $10 million, requires fewer employ-

ees and less time to print the same number of papers as the company's current equipment. This will save the company nothing in the first year, but it will generate $500,000 of cash inflow in Year 2, $3 million in Year 3, and $6.5 million in Year 4. The press's payback period, then, would be four years. Now, if the company learned that it could invest in another long-term capital project with a payback period of just two years it might opt for that instead.

But what if the comparison weren't so clear-cut? What if you had two competing $10 million capital projects with four-year payback periods—one that paid back $0 in Year 1, $0 in Year 2, $1 million in Year 3, and $9 million in Year 4; and another that paid back $1 million in Year 1, $3 million in Year 2; $4 million in Year 3, and $2 million in Year 4? Obviously, the latter project would give you access to money sooner rather than later—allowing you to invest it and to let it compound. In that sense, the latter project would actually pay back in slightly *less than* four years, since your company could have invested the $1 million it got back in Year 1 for three years; the $3 million it got back in Year 2 for two years; and the $4 million it got back in Year 3 for one year.

This point—that there is a time value of money—is a critical one, yet it is missing from payback analysis. Payback analysis fails to consider that there is more to the cost of capital than the original outlay of money. There is the original outlay of money plus the amount of interest it could have earned, based on alternative investments and *time*, had it not been used for this particular capital project.

• *Net present value analysis.* As a result of the shortcomings in payback analysis, companies rely on more sophisticated capital budgeting techniques that reflect the time value of money. One is net present value. Briefly—since your company has a capital budgeting team that deals with this very question—net present value analysis involves three steps:

   1. Your company projects the cash flow that the project will generate into the future and adjusts that to reflect the time value of money. That means the cash flow of a ten-year capital project that pays back all $10 million in Year 1 will be considerably more than the cash flow of one that pays back $100,000 in each of the following ten years.

2. Your company projects the cash outflow required of the capital project—namely, the original investment—and adjusts that to reflect the time value of money, too.

3. Your company adds up the present value of a project's cash inflows and outflow. If the number is positive—in other words, if the value of the inflow exceeds the value of the original investment—the project is worth entering into. (Obviously, there may be other reasons to enter or not to enter into a capital project than just this.)

• *Internal rate of return.* The concept of internal rate of return is somewhat simple, though it can be a nightmare to figure out without a financial calculator. In the context of capital budgeting, IRR represents that rate of return at which the present value of a project's inflow equals that of its outflow. In that sense, it is related to net present value analysis.

Perhaps this will help explain the situation: Your company establishes a so-called *hurdle rate* for all projects it is considering. The hurdle rate is simply that rate of return that a project must generate for it to be considered worth investing in. Usually, the company will factor in the rate of return it could earn in alternative investments—and the level of risk associated with a project—to set the hurdle rate. In the context of net present value analysis, the hurdle rate is that point when the net present value of inflow and outflow is greater $0. In the context of IRR, a project is considered worthwhile when the internal rate of return of the investment *exceeds* the hurdle rate of return on capital projects established by the company.

How Are Budgets Put Together?

Regardless of the type of budget you're dealing with, each is assembled in similar ways. The budgeting process requires essentially five steps:

Step 1: Determining the Flow of Information

A company gathers the data necessary to compile a budget in one of two ways: 1) It centralizes the process and has senior management establish the company's priorities

and projections; or 2) it directs individual work units and departments to assemble that information on their own. The former is referred to as *top-down budgeting*, the latter as *bottom-up*.

In general, budgets that are constructed from the *bottom up* are preferable, if only for the reason that individual workers and units know more about their departments than central management. On the other hand, bottom-up budgeting requires more time to execute and is difficult to manage.

Step 2: Deciding What You're Going to Measure

Imagine you work for Jim's Sporting Goods. But this time, imagine the company is much larger than we first described. In addition to selling basketballs, it sells baseballs and soccer balls, too. And imagine that Jim's has operations in North America, Asia, and Europe.

When Jim's prepares its budget, should it gather information based on its products? For instance, should it make separate sales and cost projections for basketballs, baseballs, and soccer balls—no matter which country they are sold in? It could do that. Or should it make projections based on its regions of operations? For instance, should it make separate sales and expense projections for its products based on whether they are sold in North America, Asia, or Europe? It could do that, too. Or should it break down its budget projections based on functions? For instance, should its marketing and manufacturing divisions assemble their own separate budgets that cover all regional operations and all products? Once again, it could.

The answer depends on how your company is organized. Or how it wants to be organized. For instance:

- If Jim's is organized in such a way that each of its products are separate *profit centers*—which means that the basketball division would be in charge of its own manufacturing, distribution, marketing, and sales functions—completely separate from the functions of the baseball and soccer ball divisions—then it will probably budget along its *product lines*.

- If the company's geographic operations are separate profit centers, sometimes called *accountability centers*, then it may choose to budget by region.

- And if the company is organized based on traditional functions—for instance, there's a separate sales department that handles all products in all regions, a separate manufacturing department that handles all products in all regions, and a separate distribution department for all products in all regions—then it may budget along these lines. The sales department, in this situation, would be referred to as a *revenue center*, while the manufacturing and distribution divisions would be considered *cost centers.*

Step 3: Gathering Historic Data

After a company decides how it will segment its operations, it turns its attention to gathering historic performance information.

The first place to look for historic performance data is the company's financial statements—its balance sheet, income statement, and cash flow statement. Another source would be the financial ratios we discussed in chapter 6. Finally, the managerial reports supplied to company executives throughout the year serve as useful tools in gathering more specific data, such as sales trends for individual products, cost trends for those products, and divisional performance.

Sales Information

When it comes to gathering historic sales data, your company ought to know its past performance based on:

GIVING YOURSELF SOME WIGGLE ROOM

When budget officers prepare a cash budget, they tend to *overestimate* expected cash outflows, or expenses, while *underestimating* inflows, or revenues. The reason? This way, should projections fall short, the company will still be able to pay its bills. In effect, budget officers do this to build in some wiggle room.

- *Product lines.* In the case of Jim's Sporting Goods, the company should know how its basketball, baseball, and soccer ball sales have done for at least one to two years, but preferably three to five years or more.

- *Regions.* Jim's should also be able to break down past sales performance based on its regions of operation. For instance, it should know how well basketballs have sold recently in North America. In addition, it should know how sales are doing in specific countries and markets.

- *Customers.* It's not enough for Jim's to know *how many* baseballs it is selling in Mexico. It needs to know *who* is buying its baseballs. For instance, what percentage of Jim's Sporting Goods sales growth is due to its contracts with large retailers as opposed to small independent stores? This information can be useful in making future projections. For instance, let's assume that the Mexican economy is headed for a recession. And large retailers have historically weathered these recessions better than small independent sporting goods stores. If Jim's sells the majority of baseballs in Mexico to large retailers, then its sales might not be altered too much based on changing economic conditions. But if the company sells the majority of baseballs in Mexico to small stores, then it might take that information into account when adjusting its forecasts for its Mexican sales—or overall sales of baseballs.

Expense Information

When it comes to gathering historic expense data, your company should know its past performance based on:

- *Direct costs.* This includes raw materials, labor, and inventory costs.

- *Indirect costs.* This includes selling, research & development, and general & administrative expenses.

- *Fixed costs.* This includes many of the indirect costs of doing business, such as rent and depreciation—which are part of G&A expenses.

- *Variable costs.* This includes many of the direct costs of doing business, such as raw materials, energy, and labor costs as well as taxes, which are also considered a variable expense.

Step 4: Making Projections

The final step in the budgeting process is for the company to project its performance for the coming year. A budget is only as good as its projections. Establishing budget projections can be as simple or complicated a task as your company makes it. For instance, some companies rely on *incremental budgeting,* in which forecasts are directly tied to past performance and are therefore easy to prepare. Others rely on *zero-based budgeting,* in which forecasts have nothing to do with past performance and are therefore more difficult to prepare. And still others rely on a hybrid approach.

Incremental Budgeting

Imagine you're preparing your company's sales budget. Last year, the company spent $10 million on newspaper advertising. How much should your company budget for newspaper ads next year?

Some companies would take that $10 million figure, and add to it an additional 10 percent—or $1 million—to factor in inflation and an acceptable level of growth in spending. This is referred to as *incremental budgeting.* Incremental budget projections are the simplest to prepare. All you need to know is what the company spent or made in the previous year. Then you tack on whatever percentage increase—or decrease—you think is appropriate.

On the other hand, the incremental approach is the least precise method for preparing a budget. Often, companies that rely on incremental budgets repeat past mistakes. Let's say Jim's Sporting Goods budgeted $1 million for general and administrative costs last year. Though the company could get by with just $750,000 this year, it budgets $1.1 million—not because it needs it, but because it is about the same amount it spent the previous year.

Zero-Based Budgeting

Zero-based budgeting is the antithesis of the incremental approach. Popularized in the 1970s, zero-based budgets operate on the premise that the amount a company budgeted for a line item in one year has little to do with what it should be budgeting in future years. While more accurate than incremental budgets, zero-based budgets require tremendous amounts of information. Thus, they are extremely time-consuming and expensive.

The Hybrid Method

Most companies rely on a hybrid approach to budgeting, in which projections are based in part on past performance. However, current industry trends and macroeconomic forces are also considered in part of the equation.

Industry Trends

The health of your industry can have a profound impact on your company's sales projections. For instance, no matter how effective your sales division is and how impressive your products are, larger developments in your industry can destroy your budget projections. Just consider what happened to restaurants that sold beef in England during the Mad Cow Disease scare of the mid- to late 1990s.

Companies turn to a variety of sources to gather this information, including:

- *Trade associations and publications.* Most trade associations publish industrywide sales and expense information based on figures provided by their members. In addition, companies like Dun & Bradstreet publish key financial ratios that can help businesses assess the health of their industries.

- *Available financial statements.* Publicly traded companies are required by the SEC to submit quarterly 10-Q reports, annual 10-K reports, and comprehensive annual reports that include financial statements. This information is primarily useful for investors, but competitors can also use it to discover broad trends in the industry.

- *Available government data.* Various agencies, such as the Commerce Department, the Agriculture Department, and the Labor Department put out regular reports on industry trends.

- *Internal experts.* Companies should also rely on their own officers who are intimately familiar with broad industry trends to contribute to this analysis.

Economic Data

The health of the economy can play a dramatic role in the health of your business, too. In fact, a number of outside influences will throw off your company's budget projections. Those include:

- *Economic downturns.* Sales projections are often predicated on a certain degree of overall economic health. A sudden recession, for instance, could reduce overall consumer demand. Local economic slowdowns can be just as devastating. Consider what happened to companies in Southern California as defense contracts were cut during the late 1980s and early 1990s. (We'll explain how this and other macroeconomic forces affect your company's finances in chapter 14.)

- *Inflation.* Even a slight increase in inflation can increase a company's expenses, from energy to raw materials to labor. Just recall the effects of hyper-inflation in the 1970s and early 1980s on U.S. industrial profits. Inflation can also dampen sales, due to increased prices.

- *Interest rates.* If the Federal Reserve raises rates, it would increase the cost of borrowing money, which would increase a company's expenses. So interest rate fluctuations should be factored into budget projections.

- *Consumer confidence.* A slight decrease in consumer confidence could hurt consumer demand, which could alter your company's sales projections.

- *Currency trends.* A sudden change in exchange rates could wipe out potential profits for multinationals, exporters, and importers.

- *Politics.* President Clinton's failed attempt at healthcare reform in 1993 boosted the short-term fortunes of HMOs, but crippled medical research companies. When making budget projections, your company ought to keep similar political issues in mind.

- *Natural disasters.* Insurers and companies that do business in disaster-prone regions must consider the potential effect of natural disasters—both positive and negative. If your company is a retailer or manufacturer, for instance, a single hurricane can wipe out a major portion of its business. If your company is a contractor, natural disasters can actually boost sales, since communities must rebuild following disasters. These days, many companies consult with independent weather services before forecasting sales and inventory trends.

- *Technology.* New technological developments can often boost or reduce demand for your products. They can also impact your costs.

- *Regulatory trends.* Businesses must also assess potential changes in the regulatory environment. That's what healthcare companies were forced to do during the healthcare reform debate of 1993. And that's what tobacco companies have been forced to do in recent years.

Step 5: Determining Your Break-Even Point

Let's say you're preparing a household budget. How do you know how much you can spend and still break even? For starters, you figure out how much you'll earn in the coming year. What do you do next? You calculate all your *variable* and *fixed costs.* *Fixed costs* are those costs that you cannot reduce based on usage. These might include your mortgage payments, car payments, and insurance payments. Variable costs are those that you can control based on usage. For instance, if you cut down your long-distance calls by 20 percent, you can reduce your phone bills. If you eat out less, you can save money on food and entertainment. If you send your youngest child to public school rather than private school, you can reduce your educational expenses. As long as your fixed costs + variable costs do not exceed your salary—or revenue—you know you will break even. This occurs when:

Net Revenue = Fixed Costs + Variable Costs

Like you, the goal of every company is to ensure that in the coming year, its fixed costs and variable costs won't exceed revenues. The process is more complicated than in a household budget, however, since a business's variable costs are interwined with its revenues.

Whereas the variable costs for our household budgets, such as groceries, have nothing to do with our revenue source (our salaries), the variable costs of a company have everything to do with its revenue source—its products. If Jim's Sporting Goods wants to increase its revenues by selling more basketballs, it will have to make more basketballs. And to make more basketballs, it will have to buy more raw materials and perhaps hire more workers.

So how does a company like Jim's know the number of basketballs it must sell to break even?

Contribution Margin

To feel for its break-even point, Jim's Sporting Goods will first determine its *contribution margin*. The contribution margin is simply the amount of money left over after variable costs are subtracted from its revenues. So, for instance, let's say Jim's Sporting Goods sells its basketballs for $10 apiece. And let's say the variable costs that go into each basketball total $6. The contribution margin on Jim's basketballs would be $4.

The reason this $4 is called the contribution margin is because it represents the amount of money left over that "contributes" to covering a company's fixed costs and profits.

Contribution Margin = Sales Price per unit – Variable Costs per unit

Break Even by Units

The contribution margin alone tells a company little about how many products it will need to sell to break even. But it is a critical component in a mathematical formula that does. This formula states that…

Break Even = Fixed Costs/(Sales Price per unit − Variable Costs per unit)

or

Break Even = Fixed Costs/Contribution Margin per unit

To explain how this formula works, lets assume that Jim's sells its basketballs for $10 each. Let's further assume that it has $2 million in fixed costs and that its variable costs amount to $6 per ball. Now, let's plug in the numbers:

Break Even = $2 million/($10 − $6)

Break Even = $2 million/$4

Break Even = 500,000

This tells us that based on its cost structure, Jim must make and sell at least 500,000 basketballs to break even.

Break Even by Sales

Another way to determine a company's break-even point is through *dollars*, not units. To determine this break-even point, Jim's can turn to another simple formula. It states that:

Break even = Fixed costs/[(Sales Price per unit − Variable Costs per unit)/Sales Price per unit]

or

Break Even = Fixed Costs/(Contribution Margin per unit/Sales Price per unit)

Once again, let's assume that Jim's fixed costs equal $2 million; its variable costs per unit is $6; and its sales price per unit is $10.

Break Even = $2 million/[($10 − $6)/$10]

Break Even = $2 million/($4/$10)

Break Even = $2 million/0.4

Break Even = $5 million

This formula tells Jim's Sporting Goods that it will achieve break even once sales of basketballs hits $5 million.

Beyond Break Even

In our example, we know that Jim's Sporting Goods will break even when it sells 500,000 basketballs. But the goal of a company is to do better than break even—it's to actually make a profit. How does a company know how much profit it will make by selling more than its break-even volume?

Simple: Let's assume that Jim's Sporting Goods, knowing that its break-even point is 500,000 basketballs, commits to selling 700,000 balls in the coming year. To figure out how much profit 700,000 basketballs will generate, all the company needs to know is its fixed costs, its variable costs, and its projected revenues.

In our example, Jim's still plans to sell its balls for $10 apiece. At 700,000 units, that's $7 million in revenues. Despite the increased production, its fixed costs remain at $2 million (after all, the definition of a fixed cost is one that does not change based on volume of activity). The company's variable costs per unit will stay the same, but its overall variable costs will rise. Based on a variable cost per unit of $6 and 700,000 basketballs, we know that Jim's total variable costs will be $4.2 million. Given the fact that profits equal revenues minus expenses, Jim's can conclude that it will make $800,000 on 700,000 basketballs.

Revenues = $7 million

Fixed Costs = $2 million

Variable Costs = $4.2 million (700,000 basketballs x $6 in Variable Costs per unit)

Profit = $7 million – $2 million – $4.2 million = $800,000

But let's say that Jim's Sporting Goods does not know how many basketballs it will make in the coming year. All it knows is that it wants to generate $1 million in profits next year. Can the company figure that out using this formula? Sure. All it would need to do is to modify it: Profit = Revenues – Fixed costs – Variable Costs. In this case, we know the intended profit: $1 million. We know that fixed costs will be the same: $2 million. We know variable costs per unit will be the same: $6. And we know how much it intends to price each basketball: $10. All we need to know is what volume of sales will generate the right level of revenues and total variable costs to achieve $1 million in profits.

Profit = (Sales Price per unit x Volume) – Fixed Costs – (Variable Costs per unit x volume)

$1 million = ($10x) – $2 million – ($6x)

$3 million = 10x – 6x

$3 million = 4x

x = 750,000

This formula tells Jim's that to make $1 million in profit, it must sell 750,000 basketballs. As you can see, cost is a critical component of profitability. We'll explain how companies account for their costs in the following chapter, which covers *cost accounting*.

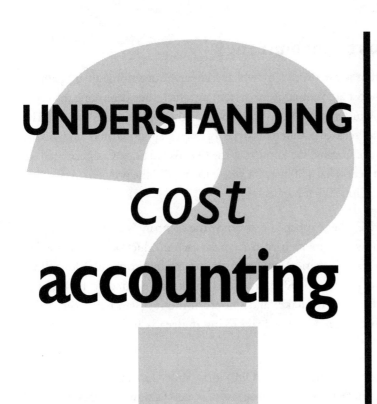

UNDERSTANDING
cost
accounting

CHAPTER EIGHT

Imagine you run your own company. Thanks to financial accounting, you know how well your company per- formed last year.

But how do you know which products to manufacture *next year?* How do you know how many units of each product your company should make? And how do you know how to price your products?

To figure this out, managers rely on an important aspect of managerial accounting: *cost accounting.*

Cost accounting is an intricate endeavor. There are entire books written on how to do it properly. One good one is *Managerial Accounting*, edited by Arthur J. Francia (Dame Publications, 1994). Our intent isn't to teach you how to be a cost accoun- tant, but rather to clue you in on some of the things cost accountants look for.

What Is Cost Accounting?

If financial accounting is the process by which companies determine their results—sales and earnings—cost accounting is the system by which they determine the *cause* of those results. For instance, let's say you work for the Old World Shoe Co. The company makes and sells two different styles of men's shoes: loafers and boots. Thanks to financial accounting, we know that the Old World Shoe Co. generated $1 million in profit last year. That's 50 percent worse than it did the previous year, when profits topped $2 million. What happened?

One way to determine what happened is to study the company's *costs*. Obviously, a company should know how much it costs to make each product before it manufactures these goods. This information helps it to: 1) determine how much to sell its product for; 2) decide if a product is worth making; 3) decide how many units of each product it will make; and 4) determine if it can make the product cheaper, or if it can get a better deal buying it already made from an-other company.

In our example, one explanation for the Old World Shoe Co.'s falling profits could be that the *cost* of manufacturing boots rose last year. Let's assume that this occurred. Without proper cost accounting, the company would not have known this fact. If the company did not know this, it wouldn't have known to raise its prices to keep pace. And that may be the very reason that the company's profits fell.

What if the problem wasn't the boots? Maybe a competitor came along and, through mass production, undercut Old World's prices for loafers by 50 percent. If this was the case, Old World probably needed to slash its prices just to keep up, forcing the company to sell its loafers at cost or below. How could cost accounting have helped Old World in this scenario? Here's one way: What if, through proper cost accounting, Old World realized that it could buy loafers cheaper than it could make them in-house? If this were the case, the company could have protected its profit margins by purchasing rather than making its own products.

As you can see, cost accounting is a critical tool for managers. By letting a company know how much it costs to make a single unit of a single product, it helps the firm know whether making that additional product is worthwhile.

It also helps a company determine its proper sales mix. Sales mix refers to how many units of each product a company sells. In our example, Old World may decide to go with a sales mix that favors boots over loafers based on costs and demand. Or, it could choose to make two loafers for every one boot it manufactures. Poor cost accounting could lead to shortages in profitable products, and stockpiles of unprofitable ones.

Cost accounting, like financial accounting, demands *consistency*. After all, just as investors must feel confident that a company's financial accounting methods are sound, a firm's managers must be absolutely sure that the information they are receiving about costs is consistent throughout different product lines. It does a manager no good if Old World Shoe uses one accounting method to cost its boots and another to cost loafers.

Unit Costs

So how do companies determine how much it costs to make a product? For starters, they take the *actual* amount of money required to manufacture a product and divide that figure by the number of units they produce. Seems simple enough.

Unit Costs = Total Manufacturing Costs / No. of Units Produced

For instance, in our example, Old World Shoe spent $365,000 making loafers last year, as shown in the table on page 114. With that money, it made 14,000 loafers. That means each loafer it made cost the company $26.07. Old World Shoe spent $475,000 making 15,500 boots. That means each boot cost the company $30.65.

WHAT ARE PRODUCT COSTS?

Product costs are all those costs associated with manufacturing a product. (For those companies that don't make the products they sell—such as retailers—product costs are limited to the cost of purchasing inventory.) They include the cost of:

• Raw Materials

• Labor

• Variable Overhead (such as electricity)

• Fixed Overhead (such as rent)

Old World Shoe Company
Unit Costs

	Loafers	Boots
Raw materials	$200,000	$300,000
Labor	100,000	100,000
Overhead—variable	25,000	35,000
Overhead—fixed	40,000	40,000
Total manufacturing costs:	$365,000	$475,000
Units made	14,000	15,500

What do these numbers tell us? They tell us that Old World Shoe must sell loafers for more than $26.07 a pair and boots for at least $30.65 a pair to clear a profit.

Should competition drive the price of loafers below $26.07, for instance, the company would know, based on its cost structure, that it may no longer be worthwhile to continue selling loafers. Or, this could be a sign that the company may want to outsource the production of loafers (that's if they can find a manufacturer with cheaper unit costs). Or, it could be a sign that the firm must not only outsource the production of its shoes but also find cheaper ways to store, sell, market, and distribute its products.

But taking the total manufacturing cost for a product line and dividing it by the number of units produced isn't the most accurate gauge of costs. For instance, when we calculated that Old World Shoe's unit cost for making loafers was $26.07 a pair, what we really calculated was the *average* cost for manufacturing loafers. Some loafers may have cost more. And some may have cost less, depending on when they were produced (and the cost of raw materials, labor, and overhead at that time).

To find a more accurate number, financial managers break down actual unit costs into two broad categories: *job costs* and *process costs*.

What's a Cost, What's an Expense, and What's the Difference?

We've been using the word *cost* throughout this chapter. Isn't *cost* the same thing as a *expense*? After all, if it *costs* a company $25 to make a shoe, don't those costs count as expenses on its P&L statement? Eventually. But according to the rules of GAAP, a company cannot record a cost as an expense until a transaction has been recorded. (Remember accrual accounting?)

What does this mean? It means that in any given year, your company's costs and expenses will differ. For instance, it could cost your company $2,500 to make 100 shoes. But it may only incur $1,500 of expenses. How? Let's say your company purchased $2,500 worth of leather to make 100 shoes, or $25 of leather per pair of shoes. But let's say your company only made 60 shoes this year. The cost of the leather used to make those 60 shoes—$1,500—would be counted as an expense on its income statement for the year. However, the remaining $1,000 worth of leather would be treated as a part of inventory, considered an asset on your company's balance sheet.

Job Costs

The unit cost method we described above may be appropriate for a company that mass produces its goods. But it's of little use to manufacturers that custom-make products.

Consider an airplane manufacturer. Unlike a carmaker that mass-assembles automobiles, airplane makers build planes to the exact specifications of their customers. For instance, American Airlines may want a slightly different seat configuration than the one United wants for the exact same model plane. Or Delta may want a slightly different audiovisual system installed for its First Class section than the one that Continental Airlines ordered. Therefore, taking the total manufacturing cost of planes and dividing by the number of planes produced would lump in the additional costs of building a plane for American Airlines with the baseline costs of building a plane for a no-frills carrier.

To come up with a more accurate number, cost accountants turn to something called *job costing.* Job costing simply refers to the act of taking the actual costs of producing a specific order of products and dividing that figure by the number of specific products made. If United Airlines, for instance, orders ten jumbo-jets—identical model planes with the exact same specifications—then the airplane maker could calculate the unit costs of making those planes by taking the total costs of making that batch of planes and dividing by ten.

Job Order Sheet

Old World Shoe Company
Manufactured For: Strauss Department Store

Product: Men's Black Dress Loafers

Quantity: 1,000   Date Started: 1/1/98
Order No. B-17   Date Due: 2/1/98

Raw materials	Date	Type	Quantity	Cost	Total
Labor	Date	Type	Hours	Cost	Total
Attributable overhead	Date	Type	Units	Cost	Total

Total manufacturing costs:

Generally, companies keep track of job costs on a job order sheet, like the one shown in our example on page 116. Obviously, job costing takes more time, effort, and money than simply dividing total costs by the total number of products made.

Process Costs

Given the added time and money required for job costing, some companies find that it's not worth the effort. For instance, consider the case of a company that bottles spring water. Whether that company sells its spring water to a small chain of health food stores or to large offices, the cost of obtaining and filtering that water remains the same. Therefore, this company does not need to cost its products on a contract-by-contract basis.

For instance, let's say you work for a spring water company that bottles water for the first two weeks of every month. That water goes to all its customers small and large. So, the company would take the total cost of filtering and bottling its water for January and divide that by the number of bottles of water it produced during that time. That would give the firm its *process unit cost.*

Variable Costs vs. Fixed Costs

Let's say you work for an automaker. And either through job costing or process costing, you figure out that your company actually spends $6,000 per car it makes. Does that mean that each new car the company makes will cost $6,000? Not necessarily.

To figure out how much each additional car will cost, you need more information: You need to know how much of your total manufacturing costs are *fixed costs* and how much are *variable.* You'll recall that fixed costs are those that don't fluctuate based on the number of units of product a company makes. For instance, no matter how many cars your company manufactures, its fac-

THE HYBRID APPROACH

Some companies elect to use *job costing* to determine the unit cost of raw materials. At the same time, they rely on process costing to determine the unit cost of labor and overhead.

tory rent will remain constant. On the other hand, variable costs are those costs that do fluctuate based on volume. The cost of raw materials, for instance, will change based on the amount of materials the company consumes.

Let's assume that your company spent $6,000,000 making 1,000 cars (that's how it came up with a unit cost of $6,000). And let's further assume that $4,000,000 of that $6,000,000 were variable costs and $2,000,000 were fixed. The company wants to know how much it will cost to make 2,000 cars. Is the answer $12,000,000 ($6,000 unit cost x 2,000 units)? No.

Here's why. Whether the company makes 1,000 or 2,000 cars, its fixed costs will still be $2,000,000. So that's our starting point. Now, we add the variable costs. When the company made 1,000 cars, the company incurred $4,000,000 in variable costs— meaning its *variable unit cost* is $4,000. So, at $4,000 a car, 2,000 cars would equal $8,000,000 in variable costs. Add $8,000,000 to $2,000,000, and the cost of building 2,000 cars is actually $10,000,000—not the $12,000,000 we assumed from the start.

Standard Costs

Whether your firm relies on job costing or process costing, the use of actual numbers to calculate unit cost has its shortcomings.

For instance, gathering actual costs:

- *Can be expensive*, as we just mentioned.

- *Takes time.* In our example, Old World Shoe would have to wait until the end of a month, a quarter, a year—or at the end of a job order to find out what its actual unit costs were. While the data may be accurate, it might not be available to managers in time for them to make quick decisions about future production and pricing.

- *May be difficult to calculate.* This is especially true for companies which manufacture multiple products in a single factory. Imagine you work for a clothing manufacturer, which makes sweaters, shirts, and pants.

How to Cut Costs

How does a company with disproportionately high *fixed* costs reduce costs? Simple. By increasing production.

Here's how it works. Imagine that your company owns a factory designed to produce 1,000 shoes per day. And let's further assume the fixed cost of keeping the factory running is $10,000 a day. That means that whether the factory makes one shoe or 1,000 shoes, it still costs $10,000 to operate the factory.

Now, imagine your company normally makes 750 shoes. Its *fixed costs per unit* would be $13.33 per shoe. So to produce 250 more shoes, it wouldn't incur any additional fixed costs. That's because the factory has *idle capacity*. Most factories have some unused capacity.

Assuming that you have a decent contribution margin (remember from chapter 7, a contribution margin equals sales minus variable costs), your company could reduce its overall unit cost by utilizing the plant's idle capacity and making 1,000 shoes.

Throughout the day, workers who assemble sweaters may also be responsible for making shirts, or even pants. How do you know exactly how much of your labor costs went into sweaters versus shirts versus pants?

As a result, companies also rely on *standard costing* to help fill these gaps.

What is standard costing? Think of standard costs as an estimate that the company comes up with, based on experience. The company establishes these estimates for costs throughout each stage of the manufacturing process: 1) the purchase of raw materials; 2) the work in progress stage; and 3) the finished goods stage. As

products flow through each of these stages, the company examines the actual cost of production to see how close the standard cost allowances are. The differences are recorded as *variances,* and these variances go a long way toward helping the company identify why certain products are more expensive to produce than they should be.

Distributing Shared Costs

It's easy to determine how much a product costs if the company you work for only makes one type of product. Similarly, it's simple to figure out how much raw materials cost your firm. You just calculate the amount of raw materials required to make a batch of products, and divide by the units produced. But what about labor? And what about overhead?

IDLE CAPACITY

According to the Federal Reserve, the nation's factories ran at 84 percent of capacity in October 1997. If a company determined, based on demand, that it could run its factories at 100 percent capacity, the additional 16 percent of output would be free of the fixed costs associated with running the factory.

That's why we often refer to idle capacity as underutilization of costs.

Figuring out how to apportion shared costs is one of the most difficult tasks for a cost accountant. At the same time, it's one of the most important.

Go back to our example. Like most companies in the real world, Old World Shoe manufactures more than one type of product. Let's assume, however, that it makes both loafers and boots in the same factory. Let's also assume that workers in that factory are responsible for making both loafers and boots. When assigning the cost of labor for loafers, how do you know what portion of the labor costs are attributable to loafers, and what portion should go to boots?

One way is through something called *activity-based costing,* or ABC. It works like this. Let's say that Old World Shoe makes 60 boots and 40 loafers on any given day. And let's say that it takes the same number of labor hours to make each shoe. That means on any given day, 60 percent of the company's labor hours are devoted to boots and 40 percent are devoted to shoes.

Assuming that total labor costs for a day total $10,000, the company can assign $6,000 in labor costs to boots and $4,000 to loafers.

The same is true for overhead. The rules of ABC simply state that you assign costs on the basis of usage—to the extent that usage patterns are ascertainable. For instance, let's assume your company's factory and equipment are used to make boots for six hours of a ten-hour workday. The remaining four hours are devoted to making loafers. Under ABC, you'd assign 60 percent of shared overhead costs to boots and 40 percent to loafers.

Remember: You cannot determine whether a product is worth making unless you know exactly how much it costs—and how much making additional units of that product will cost your firm. Only then can you determine its potential profitability.

MANAGING *your* cash *through the* YEAR

The goal of business is to make a profit. Generating sales and controlling costs put your business in a position to do just that. But future profits will do your company no good if it doesn't have enough cash **right now** to pay its bills and stay in business.

In fact, companies with no profits but a lot of cash—such as a number of high-tech startups—are often better off than cash-poor companies with profits. So it's incumbent upon your company to effectively *manage* the cash that flows into its accounts periodically throughout the year—and the cash that flows out.

At the very least, your company must ensure that at all times it has enough cash in its accounts to meet short-term obligations as they come due. After all, a business can make the most innovative products and reduce expenses through the most innovative management techniques. But if it doesn't have enough money to pay its bills, all those efforts will be for naught.

Companies Require Cash Because...

Cash is a company's most precious asset. It can be deployed in ways that fixed assets, such as land or facilities, cannot. For starters, cash can be used to meet routine, short-term obligations such as payroll, taxes, and overhead. In fact, your company needs cash to pay for expenses throughout each of the following steps in its normal operating cycle:

- *When it buys raw materials.* Obviously, your company will need cash to buy the materials necessary to manufacture its products or to deliver its services. To be sure, your company will be extended lines of credit from vendors. But to maintain those trade credits, the company must consistently pay its bills on time. Furthermore, some vendors offer discounts to companies that routinely pay their bills early.

- *When it converts those raw materials into products, through the manufacturing process.* This takes labor. And labor needs to be paid. For some companies, payroll must be met weekly. Others generate paychecks every other week.

- *When it sells products.* Marketing, too, requires cash. For instance, your firm needs cash to cover travel expenses and commissions for its sales force.

- *When it pays its bills.* Your company will need cash to pay its bills as accounts payable come due. It will also need to meet monthly overhead costs, such as rent and utilities.

Companies Desire Cash Because...

In addition, cash and so-called *near-cash investments*—like money-market mutual funds and ultra short-term bond funds, which can be liquidated quickly—may be used for longer-term, strategic purposes. Your company may use these liquid assets to:

- *Pay off long-term debts.* Based on interest rates, the bond market, and

the stock market, it may make sense for your company to pay down its long-term debt sooner rather than later. If it does, having access to cash will put your company at a competitive advantage.

- *Expand.* A company that has an internal source of capital to help finance expansion is always better off than one that must rely solely on external sources.

- *Invest.* Your company can't take advantage of interest rates, the bond market, or the stock market if it does not have access to excess cash.

- *Protect or improve its credit rating.* Banks and other lenders look to a company's current assets to judge its creditworthiness. The more cash a company has, the better it looks.

- *Prepare for emergencies.* You never know when an emergency will arise. For instance, a natural disaster may prevent a company from manufacturing or distributing its products. So, too, would a labor strike. Access to cash could help your company weather such events.

SWIMMING IN CASH

American companies today are generating more *free cash flow* than they have in the past. Free cash flow refers to operating cash flow minus capital expenditures. This lets a company know how much cash it really has on hand with which it can do anything it wants. The typical company in the Standard & Poor's Index of Industrial Stocks, for instance, generated $14.47 of *free cash flow* per share in 1996. That's four times as much as the typical company did in 1992. In fact, in 1960, companies were actually reporting *negative 10 cents* in free cash flow per share.

Too Much of a Good Thing

If cash is so vital, why do large companies today maintain *less* cash on their books than they did in the past? For instance, in 1997 the typical company in the Standard & Poor's index of industrial companies carried about 7 percent of its assets in the form of cash or cash equivalents, compared with 10 percent a decade earlier and nearly 30 percent a half century ago. Does this mean companies today are weaker than they were in the past?

Just the opposite. The goal of cash management isn't to hoard cash. In fact, having too much cash on hand can be just as dangerous as having too little. For instance, a company that has $1 million in excess cash actually stands to *lose* more than $400,000 over the course of five years. This assumes that the company could have invested that money at 7 percent a year.

So, the goal of cash management is to determine how much money a company needs based on its cash inflows and outflows, to maintain just enough, and to reduce so-called *opportunity costs* by investing the rest of the money at the highest rates possible for the longest periods possible. Depending on the economy and interest rates, your company may invest its excess cash in stocks or bonds. It may use the money for mergers and acquisitions. Or it may plow that money back into the company, especially if its return on investment ratios are strong. Companies may also purchase their own stock on the open market. In 1996, thanks to unprecedented cash flows, American companies had enough cash to buy back a record $176 billion worth of their own stock. The year before, companies bought back $99 billion worth of their own stock.

Four Steps to Proper Cash Management

To properly manage its cash, then, a company must:

1. *Determine its working capital needs.* Your company must do this to gauge how much cash is just enough.

2. *Find ways to collect money as fast as possible from customers.* The faster your company collects money owed, the sooner it can invest it. This is why investors favor companies whose Days Sales Outstanding ratios are lower than those of their peers.

3. *Find ways to delay payments to creditors.* The longer your company can hold on to its money, the longer it can invest it.

4. *Invest its excess cash soundly.*

The Bottom Line

Routinely, the American Institute of Certified Public Accountants examines how finances are being handled at companies throughout the country. In 1997, it looked at more than 650, including nearly half the companies in the Fortune 100. Here's what it found:

- It takes the average company 95 days to prepare an annual budget. The most efficient companies, the so-called world-class firms, can do it in only 60 days.

- The average finance department spends $3.55 to process a single invoice. World-class finance departments need just 35 cents.

- The average finance department spends $6.05 to handle a single expense report. World-class departments can do it for just 27 cents.

- The average finance department needs 67 cents to process a single remittance from a customer. World-class departments do the job for 4 cents.

- The average finance department spends $4.55 to track a single asset. By comparison, world-class departments do it for 64 cents.

- And while it takes the average finance department $1.91 to process each paycheck, the best companies spend just 36 cents.

Think about it. If you worked at a company with 10,000 employees who receive 26 paychecks a year, and you figured out how to lower the cost of processing a paycheck from $1.91 down to 36 cents, you'd save your company $403,000 a year.

Step 1: Determining Your Capital Needs

To determine how much working capital your company requires, it must first calculate whether its current assets will cover its current liabilities. To do this, your company relies on two of the key financial ratios we discussed in chapter 6: the *current ratio*, in which you divide a firm's current assets by its current liabilities to determine its liquidity; and the *quick ratio*, in which you subtract a firm's inventory from its current assets, then divide that figure by its current liabilities to come up with a more accurate reading of liquidity.

Current Ratio = Current Assets/Current Liabilities

Quick Ratio = (Current Assets – Inventories)/Current Liabilities

These ratios, however, are only a starting point. They tell you if a company is generally liquid. What they don't do is project when cash is expected to flow into your company and when cash is expected to flow out. For these projections, you have to go back to your company's cash budget, as described in chapter 7. But here are some quick back-of-the-envelope calculations to find out how much cash your company generally needs:

Calculate Your Inventory Conversion Period

Inventory conversion refers to the time it takes your company to convert raw materials into finished goods, and then to sell those goods to its customers. It can be determined by dividing your firm's inventory by its sales per day. (Note: Don't confuse this with inventory turnover, which is calculated by dividing sales by inventory.) For example, let's say your company's inventory is worth $10 million and it generates $100 million a year in sales, or $273,973 a day. By dividing $10 million by $273,973 a day, you find out that your company converts its inventory every 36.5 days.

Inventory Conversion Period = Inventory/Sales per day

Inventory Conversion Period = $10,000,000/$273,973 = 36.5 days

Calculate Your Days Sales Outstanding

Once you've made a sale, the Days Sales Outstanding ratio tells you how long it takes your customers to pay their bills. For instance, if your company has $15 million in receivables outstanding and generates $100 million in sales per year—or $273,973 a day—its Days Sales Outstanding would be 54.75 days.

Days Sales Outstanding = Accounts Receivable/Sales per day

DSO = $15,000,000/$273,973 = 54.75 days

Calculate How Long It Takes Your Company to Settle Accounts Payable

To find this out, divide your company's accounts payable—including trade credits and wages payable—by the cost of goods sold per day. If, for example, your firm has $10 million in accounts payable and the cost of goods sold is $75 million (or $205,479 per day), then it turns out that your firm takes 48.667 days to pay its bills.

Accounts Payable Deferral = Accounts Payable/(Cost of Goods Sold/365 days)

Accounts Payable Deferral = $10,000,000/$205,479 = 48.667 days

Calculate Your Cash Needs

Take the number of days it takes for your company to convert its inventory and add its Days Sales Outstanding. This represents how many days it takes for your company to convert raw materials into finished goods and to sell those goods—and then to receive cash for the goods it sold. In our example, the company's inventory conversion period was 36.5 days. And it took 54.75 days to receive payment on its sales. That comes out to 91.25 days.

Now, subtract the number of days it takes your company to pay *its* bills. In our example, the company deferred payments for 48.667 days. Subtract 48.667 days from 91.25, and the new figure—42.6 days—refers to your firm's total *cash conversion*

cycle. The cash conversion cycle—measured as *inventory conversion* plus *Days Sales Outstanding* minus *accounts payable deferral*—refers to the amount of time your company's cash is tied up.

Inventory Conversion Period + Days Sales Outstanding – Accounts Payable Deferral = Cash Conversion Cycle

"TIME IS MONEY"

Benjamin Franklin was the one who coined this oft-quoted phrase back in 1748 in *Advice to a Young Tradesman.* More to the point, perhaps, is that "Money Is Time."

Three Ways to Reduce the Time Your Cash Is Tied Up

To reduce the number of days your cash is tied up as a current asset, your company can do three things:

1. Speed up collections from its debtors

2. Delay payments to its creditors

3. Try to sell its inventory faster

Step 2: Collecting Payments

Imagine you work in your company's collection department. One of your responsibilities is to call customers who are behind in their payments. One day, you get on the phone and speak to a delinquent customer, who assures you not to worry because his "check is in the mail." Assuming he's telling the truth, how many days must your company wait to get the money? Hint: The answer is not the number of days it takes the Post Office to deliver the mail.

Between the time a customer puts a check "in the mail" and the time it's available for your company's use, several steps must take place. For instance:

• *Your company must receive the check.* Depending on the distance between the customer and the company, this may take as many as three days.

- *Your company must deposit the check.* It generally takes a day for your company's bank to record the check in its system.

- *Your company's bank must send the check off to the Federal Reserve Bank's processing center to clear.* This, too, can take a day.

- *The Federal Reserve processing center must direct funds from your customer's account into your company's account.* Depending on the distance between your customer's bank and your company's bank, this could take a day or two.

If it takes the Post Office three days to deliver that delinquent customer's check, seven days will have passed from the time he wrote the check to the time your company can actually access its money.

Eight Steps to Speed Up Collections

Each day your company is forced to wait represents another day of float. The term float simply refers to the time it takes your company to access its money after customers have sent in their payments. Each day of float represents another day of lost interest. In our example, your company is losing seven days of float. That's seven fewer days the company can invest its money or seven more days it must take out loans to make up for potential cash shortfalls.

REAL LIQUIDITY

Often, a more accurate gauge of liquidity than the quick ratio or the current ratio is the *current cash-to-debt ratio*. To calculate it, divide your company's *operating cash flow* by average current liabilities. This tells you if your company can pay its bills over time, rather than either at the beginning or the end of the year.

Operating cash flow refers to only that cash generated by the company's basic business. It does not include cash flow from investing or financing. This figure can be found easily on a company's cash flow statement.

Average current liabilities can be calculated by taking the current liabilities at the start of a period and adding that to the current liabilities at the end of a period and dividing by two.

Current Cash-to-Debt ratio = Operating Cash Flow /Average Current Liabilities

The Different Types of Float

- *Mail float.* This is the time it takes the Post Office to deliver a check that's been put in the mail.

- *Processing float.* This is the time it takes your company's collection department or lock box administrator to sort through payment envelopes, record vital information, and deposit checks with the Federal Reserve processing center or local clearinghouses.

- *Check-clearing float.* This is the time it takes for the Federal Reserve processing center or local clearinghouse to make funds available for use after receiving the checks.

- *Collection float.* This is the time it takes for checks mailed by your company's customers to be accessible by the firm. To calculate collection float, add mail float, processing float, and check-clearing float.

- *Disbursement float.* This is the time it takes for your company to mail its payments, and for the payments to be available for use by the firm's creditors.

Obviously, the challenge of financial managers is to reduce float in the collection process. Here are eight steps your company can take right now to speed up collections:

Prepare Invoices A.S.A.P.

The first thing your company can do is speed up paperwork wherever possible. For instance, let's say your firm's computerized billing system automatically mails off invoices to customers whenever merchandise is shipped. However, it takes two working days from the time an order is placed to the time your warehouse ships the goods. By changing its billing system to issue an invoice the day an order is placed, rather than when it is shipped, your company may be able to shave two days off the collection process.

Two days can mean an awful lot. For instance, let's assume that at any given moment, your company has $100 million in accounts receivable. And let's say it normally takes 30 days to receive payment. If you can bring that down to 28 days simply by changing your billing system, you could save your company nearly $55,600, assuming it could invest that money at 10 percent a year. That's $100 million at .0274 percent (daily interest rate) x 2 days = $55,600.

Offer Customers Incentives to Pay Sooner

Another simple method to speed up collections is to offer debtors a monetary incentive to pay sooner, rather than later. Your company can do this through positive reinforcement. For instance, it can agree to reduce interest rates on credit accounts that are paid off on time or early. Or it can use negative reinforcement. For instance, it could add penalties for late payments (although this is hard to enforce).

Let Customers Pay by Credit Card

Not only is this more convenient, but both the customer and the company can enjoy the float while the credit card issuer pays the bill. However, your firm won't recoup 100 percent of the money, due to processing fees charged by the card's issuer.

Use Preauthorized Payments

Increasingly, businesses are offering customers an option to make *preauthorized payments* directly from their checking accounts. Under this system, customers don't have to remember to write a check each month. The company is given the authority to withdraw the money directly from the account, on an agreed-upon date.

To get customers to preauthorize payments, your company may have to offer an

incentive, such as reduced rates. Phone companies, electric utilities, cable television companies, and insurers are among those companies adopting this system. This applies to consumer purchases; it won't necessarily work for larger vendors.

Rely On Electronic Fund Transfers

To move money quickly between banks and bank accounts, your company may want to rely on the electronic transfer of funds rather than paper checks. For instance, when your company deposits your paycheck into your bank account, it relies on something called the *automated clearinghouse network*. The ACH is a computerized network that allows companies to send checks electronically from one account to another. Electronic fund transfers are generally available for use by the recipient a day after authorization is given. This is about a day or two faster than the time it takes a written check to clear.

LOCK BOXES...

- Reduce mail delivery time.

- Reduce check-processing time.

- Increase the cost of check processing.

Rely On Lock Boxes

Lock boxes are among the oldest and most effective methods for speeding up payment collection.

Here's how they work: Instead of relying on a centralized collection center, your company establishes several *lock boxes*, which are Post Office boxes or private mailboxes, throughout the country. Each lock box is administered by a third-party vendor, usually a bank.

Rather than having customers mail checks to a central location, your company directs them to make payment to their nearest lock box. This generally reduces mail delivery time, or the *mail float*, by a day or two. For instance, if your company is based in Los Angeles but a number of its customers operate in New York, it might take three days or more for checks sent from the East Coast

to arrive. However, by establishing a lock box in New York and directing New York customers to mail payments there, checks will likely take only a day to reach the box.

As checks come into each box, the third-party administrator immediately posts them to a local bank account in your company's name. This can shave another day or two off the time it takes to process each check. How? The priority of the lock box administrator is to deposit the checks as soon as possible, not to update accounts receivable. In many circumstances, the lock box administrator will photocopy the checks as they come in rather than waste time processing the information. Once photocopied, the physical checks are deposited, and the photocopied images are mailed to the company's accounting office. The company then updates its accounts from the photocopied images.

Also, lock box administrators often rely on *local clearinghouses*, rather than a Federal Reserve processing center, to clear their checks. Local clearinghouses are simply networks of banks in a particular location that meet daily to physically exchange checks. The use of local clearinghouses tends to be more direct than the traditional system, in which checks are sent to a regional Federal Reserve processing center.

HOW LONG HAVE LOCK BOXES BEEN IN USE?

The lock box system was first devised by an executive with the RCA Corporation in 1947. Today, a majority of large companies rely on lock boxes to speed up collections.

Use Depository Transfer Checks

Depository transfer checks are unsigned checks used to move funds swiftly within a company. For instance, let's say your company has several lock boxes throughout the country, each tied to a local bank account in the company's name. To periodically pool the money into a central account, the company's central bank is given the authority to prepare a *depository transfer check* that authorizes payment from the local banks to the central fund without requiring an executive's signature.

Traditional Collections vs. the Lock Box System

Traditional Collection	Lock Box System
Customer mails check to Company location	Customer mails check to local P.O. box
Company receives check	Check is delivered to lock box, and is immediately deposited to a local bank account
Company deposits check in bank account	Check is cleared through a local clearinghouse
Bank sends check to Federal Reserve Bank processing center	Bank notifies company that money is available—Day 1
Processing center directs funds from customer's account into company's account	Money is available—Day 2
Bank notifies company that funds are available	Money is available—Day 3

Your Choice of Lock Boxes

Companies generally choose one of three types of lock box method. In descending order of cost, they are:

- *The report system,* in which the lock box administrator deposits each check into the company's account, but simultaneously produces computerized reports detailing each check that it mails or sends electronically to the company. These reports include the customer's name, check amount, check number, account number, invoice number, postmark date, and date of receipt.

- *The photocopying system,* in which the lock box administrator deposits each check into the corporate account, but first photocopies the front of each check, which is then sent along with the invoice to the company.

- *The envelope plan,* in which the lock box administrator deposits each check into the corporate account, but writes down the amount on each envelope, then bundles them together and mails them to the company.

Reduce the Time It Takes to Physically Handle Checks

As checks are delivered to a company's payment center, information on each check is used to update the company's accounts receivable. Some companies spend a full day or two inputting this information. If your company photocopies checks as they come in, just as lock box administrators do, it can immediately deposit the actual checks into its account while inputting the data from the copies later.

Step 3: Making Payments

When companies disburse payments, the goal is to *increase* float, rather than decrease it. After all, every day your company can hang on to its cash is another day it can earn interest on it. However, financial managers must be cautious. While the goal is to delay disbursement of cash, *late payments* can lead to fees and penalties that could easily wipe out the benefits of the float. Late payments can also adversely affect your company's ability to receive trade credits and can damage a company's credit ratings.

Four Ways to Slow Down Payments

Centralization

An easy way to slow down payments is to centralize all disbursements. This accomplishes two things: First, it allows a financial manager at company headquarters to assess when payments should be made on all checks issued by the company. This allows the manager to physically delay payments on low-priority accounts. Second, by centralizing the process, companies often gain mail float on their payments. For instance, let's say your company is headquartered in Boston, but has an office in Phoenix that oversees its Southwestern operations. A check sent from Phoenix to a vendor in Tucson may take one day to deliver. But if that check were issued from the company's Boston headquarters, it could take an additional two days to deliver and an additional day or two to clear.

ARE LOCK BOXES FOR EVERYONE?

Companies that must process a large volume of checks, or a modest volume of checks written out for large amounts, tend to benefit from lock boxes, despite their costs. Small companies, however, which don't receive that many payments and whose customers are located nearby tend to not benefit as much.

Mail Payments toward the End of the Work Week

Here's a nifty trick. Since banks are closed on weekends and mail service is limited, companies that mail their payments on Thursday or Friday can often earn two extra days of mail and/or processing float.

Pay by Credit Card at Billing Due Date

If your company is allowed to charge its payment to a credit card, it can enjoy up to 30 days of additional float. This represents the number of days between the time the credit card issuer pays the bill and the time your company must pay the credit card issuer.

Remote Disbursement

Remote disbursement is frowned upon by the Federal Reserve system and by many vendors. So it ought to be a method of last resort. Here's how it works: Let's say your company is based in Charlotte, NC, and owes money to a vendor in Atlanta. Instead of issuing a disbursement from its Charlotte location, it decides—purposefully—to issue the payment from a satellite office in San Francisco using a California account. So, for the Atlanta vendor to gain access to the funds, it must wait for the check to travel across the country. Then, its bank must send the check back across the country to clear. While not technically illegal, the Federal Reserve has declared this is an abusive practice. Furthermore, companies that rely on this tactic run the risk of damaging their relationships with their vendors.

Step 4: Investing

As you'll recall, the purpose of managing cash is to maintain *just enough* to meet your obligations—and to invest any excess. Before deciding

ZERO BALANCE ACCOUNTS

A *zero balance account,* or ZBA, is a type of checking account that companies use to disburse payments. As the name indicates, the purpose of this account is to maintain a $0 balance. How does it work? Let's say your company writes a check for $10,000 to a vendor from one of its zero balance accounts. When the check is presented by the vendor's bank to the ZBA, $10,000 will be electronically transferred from a master account held by the company to the ZBA. Once the check clears, the vendor will receive $10,000 and the account will return to $0. ZBAs allow companies to maintain *exactly enough cash* in their checking accounts to cover specific expenses. The remainder can be held in a master account that is invested for longer periods of time at higher returns.

how to invest that money, though, your company must first determine how much money it has to invest—and how long that excess money will be available. The amount and time will dictate where the money should be put.

How Much Cash Do You Have to Stash?

To gather this information, your company relies on its cash budget. As you'll recall from chapter 7, cash budgets indicate how much cash a company is expected to have at the beginning of each month; how much cash is expected to flow in; how much cash is expected to flow out; and what the company's cash position is expected to be at the end of the month. Take a look at the hypothetical cash projections for Allied Auto Parts, Inc. on the next page.

FOUR STEPS TO PROPER CASH MANAGEMENT

- Step 1: Determine working capital needs.

- Step 2: Find ways to collect money faster from customers.

- Step 3: Find ways to delay payments to creditors.

- Step 4: Invest excess cash properly.

Where Should You Stash Your Cash?

In addition to how much money a company has to invest and how long it has access to those funds, where a company invests depends largely on its own tolerance for risk. For instance, the board of directors of some companies may restrict it from investing in bonds that aren't *investment grade*. Investment grade bonds are rated by credit agencies as BBB (which means adequate) or higher.

Cash to be held for short-term obligations can be held in the form of cash equivalents or near-term cash reserves. Some examples of appropriate investments are:

- *Treasury bills.* These ultra-safe investments typically mature in three months to a year. In December 1997, they yielded between 5 and 5.5 percent annually.

Allied Auto Parts, Inc.—Cash Projections

	Cash at Beginning of Month	Cash Inflow	Cash Outflow	Available at Month's End
Jan.	$2,000,000	$750,000	($900,000)	$1,850,000
Feb.	1,850,000	800,000	(850,000)	1,800,000
March	1,800,000	650,000	(575,000)	1,875,000
April	1,875,000	345,000	(675,000)	1,545,000
May	1,545,000	375,000	(650,000)	1,270,000
June	1,270,000	400,000	(500,000)	1,170,000
July	1,170,000	475,000	(490,000)	1,155,000
Aug.	1,155,000	678,000	(567,000)	1,266,000
Sept.	1,266,000	875,000	(673,000)	1,468,000
Oct.	1,468,000	1,750,000	(750,000)	2,468,000
Nov.	2,468,000	1,800,000	(825,000)	3,443,000
Dec.	3,443,000	2,000,000	(1,345,000)	4,098,000

- *Money-market mutual funds.* Companies can immediately liquidate their holdings in these funds. In December 1997, they were returning about 5 percent a year.

- *Ultra-short-term bond funds.* Companies can immediately liquidate their holdings in these funds. In December 1997, some of the best performing ultra-short-term bond funds were returning 6 to 7 percent annually.

Three Safeguards Against Fraud

- *Maintain rigid hiring standards,* especially for employees in charge of handling collections and disbursements.

- *Pay by check.* This way, all payments can be matched up with bank statements to assure the legitimacy of each transaction.

- *Deposit payments immediately.* If cash and other forms of payment are always deposited on the day of delivery, dishonest employees will have less opportunity to access the funds.

- *Certificates of deposit.* CDs can be liquidated immediately, but there may be a penalty charged for early withdrawal. In December 1997, they were yielding about 5 percent a year.

The remainder of the cash should be put into higher-returning securities, such as:

- *Stocks.* Though the stock market can be volatile, equities as a class have yielded 10.7 percent a year, on average, since 1926. Your company can invest in its own shares—called share buybacks—or it can invest in shares of other companies.

- *Treasury notes.* These instruments mature in 3 to10 years. In December 1997, they were yielding 5 to 6 percent a year.

- *Treasury bonds.* These instruments mature in 10 to 30 years. In December 1997, they were yielding around 6 percent a year.

- *Corporate bonds.* In December 1997, high-quality corporate bonds were yielding 6 to 8 percent a year.

- *Municipal bonds.* AAA-rated state and local government bonds were yielding roughly 5 percent a year in December 1997. But interest on these bonds is not subject to federal taxes. Therefore, their *taxable equivalent yield*—the yield that a taxable bond would have to deliver to equal its return—was roughly 7 percent.

As important as cash is, it is only one asset that your company must manage. Proper financial management also entails the effective management of credit and inventory, too. We'll address those assets in the following two chapters.

MANAGING
credit
without
FEAR

CHAPTER TEN

You've probably seen the spectacle: A home electronics store advertises a year-end blowout sale, declaring, "You can buy a $2,000 giant-screen television for no money down, and no interest payments for the next 12 months!"

A one-year interest-free loan? Are they crazy? Maybe. Maybe not.

Conceptually, the company is doing what all businesses that extend credit do: It is attempting to move inventory a little faster—and to move a little more inventory. You'll recall from the previous chapters that there are three basic ways for companies to reduce their requirements for cash. They can: 1) speed up collections; 2) delay payments; or 3) increase the speed with which sales are made. We've discussed the first two already. One way your company can do the third is through strategic credit management.

What Is Credit?

When a company extends credit, it is in essence providing a loan to customers. For instance, when that home electronics store advertises a no-money down, no-interest credit special, it is offering a cheap loan to customers who don't have $2,000. The same is true for suppliers who provide *trade credit* to businesses. In this relationship, the supplier is extending a 30-day, no-interest loan in exchange for getting your company's business. Today, credit is a necessity. It must be extended to attract customers.

THE LAWS OF CREDIT

A loose credit policy tends to...
- Increase sales.

- Increase days sales outstanding.

- Increase collection costs.

A tight credit policy, on the other hand, tends to...
- Reduce sales.

- Reduce days sales outstanding.

- Reduce collection costs.

How Do Companies Manage Credit?

Managing credit involves two basic steps. The first step is deciding who your company should offer credit to. In addition, what should the terms of that credit be? The second step involves managing the *accounts receivable* that are established as a result of extending that credit. In many respects, this step is similar to managing cash.

Step 1: Establishing Credit Standards

Each company will determine, based on its relationships with its customers and its own needs, how liberal or conservative to be when it comes to extending credit. But all companies rely on some system to determine who should be eligible for these loans, and who should not.

If yours is a large and sophisticated concern, it may rely on statistical methods, such as Multiple Discriminant Analysis, or MDA.

MDA works something like this: Let's say your company sells lug wrenches to 100 auto repair shops. Historically, about 80 of those shops have paid for supplies on time. The other 20, however, have been delinquent. Using MDA, your company would attempt to find similarities among the 20 delinquent shops. For instance, it may discover that the one thing that the 20 delinquent shops have in common is that their debt-to-equity ratio is 20 percent worse than their industry peers. Or perhaps all 20 score terribly when it comes to the acid test, otherwise known as the quick ratio. Your company then does the same thing with the 80 shops that aren't delinquent.

Then, based on its findings, it creates a *credit scoring* system. The higher a company's income, for instance, the greater it might score in this system. The higher its debts, however, the lower it would score. Your company then decides what a minimum score must be for a customer to be awarded credit.

The benefit of such a system is that large companies that don't have relationships with their customers can determine whom to extend credit to without much effort. Of course, such a system has its flaws. For instance, without ever meeting customers face-to-face—and without talking to their banks and other creditors—your firm may never really know whether or not a company is honorable enough to pay back the loan.

The Five C's of Credit

Whether your company relies on a system like MDA or uses a qualitative method to determine who is creditworthy, it ought to take the following considerations into account. These are known as the five C's of credit:

- *Character.* Does this customer have a history of honoring its debts? One way to find this out

CONDITIONAL CREDIT

If your company sells big-ticket items—such as heavy machinery—to customers on installment plans, it may want to use a **conditional sales contract.** Under a conditional sales contact, your client has use of the product, but your firm maintains ownership until final payment is made. This way, should customers fail to satisfy their credit terms, your firm can reduce its losses by reclaiming the merchandise.

is to ask the customer's other creditors, such as banks or suppliers. Some companies have bond ratings. This, too, is a useful source for gauging character, since bond rating agencies routinely check companies' credit histories. You can also turn to credit reports. Dun & Bradstreet, for instance, issues credit reports on businesses that indicate their payment history and the amount of credit that companies currently have outstanding. Consumer credit companies, such as Equifax and TransUnion, publish similar reports on individuals.

- *Capacity.* Does the customer already rely on too much credit? If it does, then there's a good chance that it might not be able to pay back its debts in a timely fashion. Good sources for this information include credit reports—once again Dun & Bradstreet—and the company's own financial statements. The income statement, for instance, will indicate annual debt repayment obligations. And the balance sheet will show overall debt.

- *Capital.* What are the customer's financial resources? You can request a customer's bank account information to find this out. You can certainly conduct a background check on the company through credit reports. And you can rely on its balance sheet.

- *Conditions.* Is the customer's business in an unstable economic or political region?

- *Collateral.* Does the customer have unsecured assets that it can use to back up the debt?

The Benefits of Loose Credit

What if your company decides to relax its credit standards? When a company *loosens* its credit policies, it can do one or both of the following: 1) extend credit to a greater number of customers; or 2) improve the terms of the credit it is willing to extend to customers.

Both of these moves are likely to improve sales—at least in the short term.

Let's go back to our example of the home electronics store. Let's say you take the company up on its offer and agree to buy that $2,000 giant-screen TV. While you won't have to make interest payments for the next 12 months, you will have to make monthly payments on the principal. So, let's assume that at the end of 12 months, you pay for the set—interest free. If the actual cost of goods sold on that television was $1,000 and the cost of extending credit represented another $500, the company still made $500 profit on the set based on the $2,000 you paid for it. That's despite the interest-free loan it floated to you. In this scenario, the company believes that earning a $500 profit today is better than $1,000 later.

...and the Hazards

But what happens if, after taking possession of the TV, you miss several monthly payments? That could throw off the company's cash flow. Or what if you default on the loan? That could throw off the company's profit. In our example, if you fail to pay back the home electronics store, not only will the company be out the $500 profit it had booked. It will also have to *spend* money trying to recoup its money or take a loss on the inventory.

For loose credit policies to work, then, companies must be assured of three things:

• The policy will boost sales enough to cover the expense of the credit.

THE COSTS OF CREDIT

Offering credit costs your firm money. These costs include:

• The cost of capital (while your company's money is tied up in accounts receivable)

• The cost of hiring personnel to manage credit accounts

• The cost of the computer systems needed to maintain those accounts

• The cost of collection agencies that may be required to assist in the collection process

Setting a Collection Policy

Once your company establishes its credit policy, it must decide how it will handle delinquent accounts. Your company must determine:

- *...if and when it will send a letter to remind customers of past due accounts.* Many companies automatically issue a reminder note ten days after the official due date has passed.

- *...if and when it will call delinquent customers.* Many firms call customers once their accounts are close to being 60 days past due.

- *...if and when it will rely on collection agencies to help recoup its money.* Some companies hire collection agencies to handle accounts once they go three months past due. However, this costs money (collection firms often charge fees and/or take a percentage of the money they recover). Furthermore, your company risks angering customers by relying on these agencies.

- *...at what point your company will decide to write off certain accounts receivable as "uncollectible."* Companies routinely write off these assets and expense them against the current year's income statement—figuring that it is no longer worth the money and time to try to collect the debt.

- Customers who are extended credit can be trusted to pay back their loans.

- The policy will not make customers dependent on credit.

Step 2: Managing the Receivables

It is not unusual for companies to have a quarter or even half of their assets tied up in accounts receivable. Managing these receivables is similar to managing cash. Regardless of whether the actual credit policy is *loose* or *tight*, the credit manager's job is to speed the collection of debt. Companies rely on several techniques for this:

Days Sales Outstanding

The first thing your company does is monitor its *days sales outstanding* ratio. As we've mentioned, this ratio measures how quickly customers are paying their bills. The DSO can be calculated by taking a company's accounts receivable and dividing that by sales per day.

Days Sales Outstanding = Accounts Receivable/(Sales/365)

Assuming your company has $10 million in accounts receivable and generates $500,000 in sales per day, its DSO would be 20 days. That means your customers tend to pay their bills within 20 days. It's useful to monitor DSO ratios over time and to compare them to industry averages.

THE PROBLEM OF HAVING TOO MUCH CREDIT

According to figures published in *Money Magazine*:
- The typical American adult held nine credit cards in 1997.

- The typical American adult's combined credit card balances totaled roughly $4,000.

- Credit card delinquencies are near 20-year highs.

- Consumer debt in 1997 reached $1.2 trillion. Roughly half of that, or $520 billion, consisted of credit-card balances and other forms of revolving credit.

Account Maintenance

Your company maintains a separate account receivable for each of its customers. Included in this account is the amount of credit outstanding and the age of the debt. For instance, if Strauss' Department Store owes Playtown Toys for inventory, then Playtown ought to know how old the debt is and when the bill will become past due.

On the day the account becomes delinquent, Playtown's computer system should be set up to notify the company of the delinquency. Playtown may choose to mail letters to Strauss' reminding it of its obligation at this point. Or it may choose to call its managers directly. In fact, many companies have designed their computers to place routine reminder calls to customers every other day or so while the account remains delinquent.

Aging Schedules

Information from individual receivables accounts is posted to an *aging schedule*. An aging schedule, such as the one shown here, indicates how many days a company's accounts receivable have been outstanding.

Playtown Toys
Aging Schedule

Age of Accounts Receivable	Value	Percent of Total Accounts	Industry Average
0-10 days	$1,500,000	11	15%
11-20 days	4,000,000	31	25
21-30 days	6,000,000	47	55
31-45 days	750,000	6	3
46-60 days	500,000	4	1
Over 60 days	100,000	1	1
Total	$12,850,000		

Playtown's aging schedule shows that 42 percent of its accounts are outstanding for less than 20 days. That's slightly better than the industry average. However, 11 percent of its accounts are delinquent, compared with just 5 percent for the industry.

Incentives

As we mentioned in the previous chapter, companies use discounts to get customers to pay their bills *early*. For instance, companies often extend favorable credit terms to businesses willing to pay their bills in ten days or less. Let's say Playtown Toys agrees to supply toys to Strauss' Department Store. To get Strauss' to clear its trade credit early, Playtown may extend it credit terms of 2/10 net 30. That's shorthand. Playtown is letting Strauss' know that it is willing to give it a 2 percent discount if it pays its bill within ten days. The *net 30* refers to the fact that the full payment is due in 30 days.

MANAGING *your* own INVENTORIES

CHAPTER ELEVEN

Imagine this scenario: You work for Strauss' Department Store. Last year, Strauss' got caught short-handed. During the holiday shopping season, it failed to stock enough Star Wars merchandise to meet demand.

When December rolled around, customers were willing to pay 30 percent, 40 percent, even 50 percent more for the toys than their suggested retail price. But since Strauss' ran out by November, its customers were forced to go elsewhere. As a result, this year, Strauss' decides to carry twice as much Star Wars merchandise as it did the year before. What's more, to ensure that it has first crack at the most popular toys, it commits to buying the goods from suppliers in June—six months before Christmas. Sounds like a good idea, right?

Well, October rolls around and a new Star Trek movie hits the theatres. It becomes a blockbuster. All of a sudden, the hottest toys are based on Star Trek, not Star Wars. In November, as they begin their Christmas shopping, Strauss' customers find mer-

chandise that they don't want. So they head over to the competition, just like the year before. Strauss' not only loses sales, but it's left holding tens of thousands of dollars' worth of Star Wars toys that no one seems to want.

Now, imagine scenario number two: You work for Phil's Grocery Store. Phil's is the largest supermarket in town. Over the course of the year, Phil's notices that its customers' tastes have changed. Phil's shoppers are buying less canned goods and non-food items, while purchasing more gourmet food. So, in June, Phil's decides to cut back the amount of canned foods and consumer products it stocks by a third. In July, the National Weather Service issues a warning: This year, the town could be hit by torrential thunderstorms and perhaps even a hurricane or two. The townspeople begin to flock to the stores, in search of canned goods, batteries for their flashlights and radios, and bottled water. But because Phil's cut those inventories by a third, its customers must go elsewhere. Phil's loses out on thousands of dollars of sales.

What do these scenarios have in common? They both portray how difficult it is to manage inventory. In the first example, Strauss' loses because it *overstocks* products that customers don't want. In the second case, Phil's loses because it *understocks* merchandise that its customers do want.

What Is Inventory?

Inventory is an asset, like cash. We tend to think of inventory as just those things that companies sell. But assets that are used to make the products that companies sell are part of a company's inventory, too. If you work for a manufacturing firm, your company probably separates its inventory into three categories:

- *Raw materials.* Raw materials are the resources necessary to manufacture products. Included in this category are basic materials such as lumber or steel, in addition to component parts, such as switches and electrical devices.

- *Work in progress.* This includes unfinished products that have been worked on by labor. For instance, Boeing sells airplanes, not airplane wings. However, in the process of making those planes, the company

must also make wings. Even though the wings aren't for sale, they are still an asset to the company and therefore must be counted in its inventory.

- *Finished goods.* These are the products that companies actually sell.

Some companies, however, don't make the products they sell. For instance, a retailer simply buys ready-made goods from suppliers. In this case, the retailer only carries one type of inventory: *finished goods.*

Made-to-Order Inventory

Finished goods can be broken out into two categories. One is finished goods that are *made-to-order.* What this means is that a company converts raw materials and unfinished products into finished goods—or buys finished goods from suppliers—only *after* a customer places an order. An enginemaker, for instance, might not construct an actual airplane engine until the planemaker has placed an order and specifications have been drawn up. Similarly, an interior design firm might not order Persian rugs from its vendors until customers sign contracts to have their houses redone.

There are certain advantages to inventories that are made to order. For instance, a made-to-order system requires companies to keep less inventory in stock. This frees up a company's cash, which can be used for more strategic purposes. Second, made-to-order inventory rarely goes to waste. In our example, we noted how Strauss' Department Store was left carrying tens of thousands of dollars' worth of Star Wars toys that no one wanted. That would never occur in a made-to-order inventory system.

However, the made-to-order system can be slow and inefficient. For instance, equipment and labor would be left idle while the company waits for customers to place orders. What's more, the vast majority of companies can't get away with made-to-order inventory methods because of the rapid and recurring nature of their business. For instance, how would you react if you went to the grocery store and the clerk told you that you'd have to place an order for a can of beans and come back the following week to pick it up?

Made-to-Stock Inventory

As a result of the limitations of made-to-order inventory, companies that deal with customers en masse make finished goods that are *made-to-stock*. What this means is that their factories convert raw materials into finished goods—or the company buys finished goods—*before* customers place their orders. The finished goods are then placed in a warehouse or showroom waiting to be bought.

Made-to-order inventory management is generally safe. You know exactly how many products you need based on what your customers have ordered. Made-to-stock inventories, however, are much trickier to manage.

How Much Inventory Should You Stock?

Think of made-to-stock inventory management as a bet. To determine how much inventory to maintain in stock, your company considers several factors:

- Current customer demand

- Anticipated trends in consumer demand

- The health of the local, national, or international economy

- Anticipated trends in the local, national, or international economy

- The current cost of raw materials and labor

- Anticipated costs of raw materials and labor

- Storage capacity and costs

- Seasonal concerns

- Technology

- Competing uses of cash

- Inflation

Your company then projects sales for the coming year. When your company spends cash to make or buy inventory, it is *wagering* that its sales projections are, indeed, accurate. The cost of the bet? The money spent to make or buy the goods—in addition to the opportunity costs of what that cash could have generated had it not been tied up in inventory.

The Risks of Having Too Much Inventory

Conventional wisdom says inventory ought to be managed like cash. What this means is that companies must determine exactly how much inventory they need—and stock *just enough*. Indeed, for the past decade, American businesses have struggled mightily to reduce inventories. In 1997, for example, the typical U.S. manufacturer held just 1.2 months' worth of inventory in stock. That's 20 percent less than it did in 1993, and 40 percent less than in 1990. These efforts have freed up approximately $82 billion in extra cash.

Still, while 57 percent of U.S. companies have lowered their inventories, 43 percent are carrying the same amount—or even more—than they did five years ago, according to a recent survey by the consulting firm KPMG Peat Marwick and the University of Tennessee. What's the harm in overstocking? Overstocking can lead to:

- *Illiquidity.* Ironically, the reason companies ought to manage inventories like cash is because inventory is *not* like cash. It's less liquid. Tying up too much cash in raw materials, work in progress, or finished products could be detrimental to your company's cash flow.

- *Markdowns.* Companies that overstock must generally mark down their prices to move merchandise. For instance, fashion is constantly changing. A retailer that stocks too much of last year's styles won't be able to move that merchandise—unless it slashes prices. Obviously, this cuts into profits. On the days immediately following Christmas, you can tell which stores overstocked inventories based on the after-Christmas sales. A store that has to slash prices 40 percent, 50 percent, even 60 percent clearly got it wrong.

- *Obsolescence.* Overstocking is an especially dangerous proposition for technology-oriented companies. For instance, imagine you work for a computer maker that overstocked PCs that ran on Intel's 486 microprocessing chip. Once PCs with Pentium or Pentium II chips hit the market, all of those extra computers in your warehouse became virtually worthless.

The Risks of Having Too Little Inventory

Understocking can be just as dangerous. If your company understocks its inventory, it runs the risk of:

- *Missing out on sales.* A company cannot sell what it does not have in stock. Our example with Phil's Grocery Store illustrates this point.

- *Missing out on favorable prices.* On occasion, companies can secure better prices by buying sooner rather than later. For instance, starting in 1994, coffee companies that didn't build up their inventories paid for it dearly as coffee prices soared—more than doubling in the subsequent three years. In some cases, having *just enough* inventory is tantamount to having *too little.*

- *Missing out on discounts.* Often, companies that buy raw materials, component parts, or finished products in large quantities can secure discounts from their suppliers. Companies that stock too little or even *just enough* of these goods run the risk of missing out on these price breaks. Also, companies that place large orders infrequently, rather than small orders frequently, can reduce shipping and clerical costs.

- *Losing consumer loyalty.* If your company consistently understocks what customers want, it runs the risk of losing their future business.

Ordering Inventory

In addition to knowing how much inventory to stock, your company must also determine how much inventory to purchase at a time. For instance, there are those who believe companies ought to place several small orders for inventory throughout the year, rather than one large order. Obviously, by placing several small orders, your company can monitor its use of inventory as the year progresses and order just enough. However, the incremental approach tends to be more expensive.

To figure out exactly how large an order to place, your company probably relies on something called the *economic ordering quantity* model, or EOQ. EOQ works under a simple premise: Some of the costs associated with purchasing inventory rise as the size of the purchase rises, while others fall. For instance, if you run a bookstore and order 1,000 books as opposed to your normal 500, your total costs will rise. But some costs, like the paperwork involved in placing the order, will likely fall. After all, you're ordering 1,000 books on one invoice, instead of having to rely on two.

BUILDING IN CUSHION

Despite concerns about overstocking inventory, many companies order a few more finished goods than are necessary. They refer to these as *safety stock*. Safety stock offers some protection should there be delays in future inventory deliveries, or if some of the goods in stock are damaged.

To use EOQ, you must first determine what your fixed and variable costs are for inventory. And you need to know how many units of inventory the company sells each year.

Carrying Costs

Carrying costs represent the variable costs of ordering inventory. That means these costs—which include the cost of capital, handling costs, taxes, and depreciation—rise or fall depending on the size of the order.

Let's say you work for Strauss' Department Store. Assume the company sells 100 bicycles a year, and that each bike costs $100. This means the average inventory is worth $10,000. What are the carrying costs? Well, let's assume that it costs $1,000 to store the bikes including their share of rent, utilities, and other overhead expenses. The company must also insure the merchandise. That costs an additional $750.

Plus, at various times during the year, the company is forced to mark down its prices, as the values of the bikes erode. Let's assume this costs the company $1,000. Finally, there's the *cost of capital* invested in the bikes. Cost of capital refers to what the cash used to purchase the bikes could have earned had it been invested in something other than inventory. In other words, it represents the *opportunity costs* associated with purchasing inventory. For this example the cost of capital is 7 percent, or $700, given the fact that the bikes are worth $10,000.

When we add the figures together, we arrive at carrying costs of $3,450.

Ordering Costs

Every time a company places an order for inventory, it incurs administrative expenses, such as the cost of processing invoices and the cost of taking delivery. These are the *ordering costs* of inventory, and they tend to be fixed. That means whether you order one bike or 1,000, these costs will remain pretty much the same. In our example, let's assume that Strauss' incurs $150 in these fixed costs every time it places an order with its suppliers.

Total Inventory Costs

Combine *carrying costs* with *ordering costs* and you arrive at a company's *total inventory costs*. In our example, Strauss' total inventory costs are $3,600.

Carrying Costs + Ordering Costs = Total Inventory Costs

$3,450 + $150 = $3,600

EOQ

Now we have enough information to calculate Strauss' EOQ. EOQ is a mathematical formula that determines the optimal units of inventory that ought to be purchased per order, based on ordering costs, carrying costs, and the number of units of inventory the company sells per year. It can be expressed as follows:

$$EOQ = \sqrt{[2(F)(S)/C]}$$

F = Fixed, or Ordering Costs

S = Units of Inventory Sold per year

C = Carrying Costs per unit, in *dollar* terms

Let's plug in the numbers from our example to see how this equation really works. First, we know that F, or ordering costs, equals $150. Our carrying costs are $3,450, but we must divide that by 100 bikes to determine carrying costs per unit. When we do that, we come up with a C of $34.50. Finally, we know that Strauss' sells 100 bikes per year. So...

$$EOQ = \sqrt{[2(150)(100)/34.5]}$$

$$EOQ = \sqrt{869.6}$$

$$EOQ = 29.49$$

This tells us that the optimal number of bikes to purchase per order is about 29 or 30, based on all of the costs associated with purchasing and maintaining inventory.

EOQ can also be calculated with a slightly different formula. It states that:

$$EOQ = \sqrt{[2(F)(S)/(C)(P)]}$$

F = Fixed, or Ordering Costs

S = Units of Inventory Sold per year

C = Carrying Costs as a *percentage* of the value of inventory

P = The Price the company pays per unit of inventory

Let's go back to our example to see how this works. We know that F, or ordering costs, are still $150. S equals the company's sales (in units) per year. In this case, we know that to be 100 bikes. C equals carrying costs as a *percentage* of the value of the

inventory. In our case, Strauss' carrying costs for $10,000 worth of bikes was $3,450, or 34.5 percent. Finally, P equals the price the company pays per bike, which in this case is $100. So...

$$\text{EOQ} = \sqrt{[2(\text{F})(\text{S})/(\text{C})(\text{P})]}$$

$$\text{EOQ} = \sqrt{[2(150)(100)/(0.345)(100)]}$$

$$\text{EOQ} = \sqrt{30{,}000/34.5}$$

$$\text{EOQ} = \sqrt{869.6}$$

$$\text{EOQ} = 29.49$$

Inventory Management Is an Art, Not a Science

According to Strauss' EOQ analysis, it should order bikes in lots of 29 or 30. But what if Strauss' supplier agrees to give it a 20 percent *discount* on the bikes—or charge $80 per bike as opposed to $100—if it buys all 100 at a time? Obviously, the company must incorporate that discount into its decision-making calculus.

Or, what about this? EOQ analysis is predicated on the assumption that inventory moves in a consistent and predictable way. Even if we were to assume that Strauss' has historically sold bikes at a consistent pace throughout the year, what happens in an anomalous year? What if this year, instead of selling two bikes a week throughout the year—as it has in the past—the company sells bikes in an indiscriminate pattern? For instance, what if it sells ten bikes the first week of the year, no bikes for the next 50 weeks, and 80 bikes in the last week? In this case, it might not make sense to buy bikes in lots of 30.

There are still other considerations. What happens if skateboards are the hot commodity this year, not bikes? Though Strauss' EOQ calculation says it ought to buy 29 or 30 bikes the next time it places an order, it may choose to shrink the order—to wait and see how the new skateboarding craze will affect bike sales—before it commits that much capital.

As you can see, managing inventory is really an art form, not a science.

How to Keep Track of Your Inventory

You've probably seen this image before—perhaps the last time you went to the mall: A small store closes its doors for a day as its employees physically take count of all the merchandise it has in stock. Ideally, that company ought to know how much inventory it has at all times. But for some companies—in particular, small ones—it's difficult to do. For starters, many companies have too many products on their shelves or in their warehouses for employees to physically keep track of each day. Also, even though technology exists that can keep track of inventory on a *perpetual basis*, many small companies can't afford it. In lieu of that technology, you can imagine how inefficient it would be for some companies, such as a bookstore with 100,000 titles in stock, to physically count inventory every day.

FOUR WAYS TO KNOW WHEN TO REORDER:

- The slip method

- The line method

- The two-bin method

- Computer technology

The Periodic Method

Companies that take inventory like the store in our example are relying on a *periodic* system of inventory control. That means they only have a clear sense of what's in stock on a periodic basis.

Imagine you own a bookstore. You shut the store down for a day to check what's in stock. You learn that you have 20 copies of John Steinbeck's *Of Mice and Men*. That seems like plenty. A week passes. Do you need to order more copies of *Of Mice and Men?* Chances are no. But what if, during the week, 20 students from a local college came into the store to buy copies of the book for a class? Using periodic inventory control, you might not know that you need to reorder the book. And that's only a week after you counted.

To be sure, companies that rely on periodic inventory control do have simple ways to remind them that they should replenish their stock. Bookstores, for instance, might slip a piece of paper in between books in a stack. When the stack gets toward the bottom and the paper comes to surface, the staff will know that it's time to order more copies of a particular title.

There are other, primitive ways to gauge when inventories must be reordered, under periodic inventory control. They include the *line method* and the *two-bin method*. Under the line method, a company puts its stock in a container. For instance, a company that manufactures nails might put its finished products into a container with a line drawn around it, about a third of the way up from the bottom. As it sells nails, it takes them out of the container. When enough nails are sold and the pile drops down to a point where the line is showing, the company knows it has reached the *reorder point.*

The two-bin method is similar. In this case, a nail manufacturer might put its finished nails into two separate bins. As it sells nails, it removes them from bin one. When bin one is empty, the company knows to start making more nails. In the meantime, it sells nails from bin two.

The Perpetual Method

To avoid the use of such primitive inventory control methods, many companies rely on *perpetual* inventory control.

What is perpetual inventory control? A good example can be found at the grocery store. Most grocery stores rely on scanners. The scanners are designed to read bar codes that are affixed to each product in

THE PROS AND CONS OF JUST-IN-TIME

While just-in-time inventory control helps companies maintain their liquidity, some companies that have used it have been burned. For instance, newspaper companies that purchased newsprint back in 1993 on a just-in-time basis saw prices more than double over the course of the next two years. Therefore, by stocking *just enough* inventory, they were forced to buy newsprint at higher costs. It's also a problem if something "takes off," as when Oprah announces her book club selection.

the store. So, for instance, whenever you buy a can of soda, it is passed over the scanner, which in turn tells the cash register how much that soda costs. Simultaneously, the cash register notifies the store's master computer that a can of soda has just been purchased. All management has to do, then, is program the computer to alert it when enough soda has been sold that it must reorder. The reorder point depends on how many sodas the company believes it should have on hand at all times. At the end of each day, the store's computer system can update management on how many of each product the store sold and which products are nearing their reorder point.

Perpetual inventory does not rely exclusively on computers, though. Perpetual inventory can be done manually or with less sophisticated devices. Companies that rely on manual methods may, on occasion, use periodic physical counts as well to determine how accurate their perpetual inventory counts are.

OUTSOURCING

Outsourcing often helps manufacturers maintain just-in-time inventories. For instance, let's say a carmaker manufactures its own steering wheels. If it wanted to implement just-in-time inventory control, it would have to find a way to synchronize its steering wheel production with its assembly line so that just enough steering wheels enter the factory floor when they are needed. This can be tricky. By outsourcing the steering wheels, though, the burden of delivering the products to the factory floor just in time would fall to the supplier.

Just-In-Time

As technology improves, so, too, does the ability of business to control inventory. For instance, these days computers can update companies when inventory needs to be replenished in real time—not just at the end of the day. This is called *just-in-time* inventory control.

Over the past decade, large companies have flocked to this extremely complicated and costly perpetual system of inventory control, which factors in the speed with which a company manufactures goods or sells them. Based on the speed with which an assembly line is moving, for instance, just-in-time can tell a company to bring in more component parts to the factory, hours or even minutes before they must be

used in the assembly process. The Toyota Motor Co. was one of the first companies to perfect just-in-time more than a decade ago. Today, according to a recent survey, 71 percent of U.S. manufacturers have adopted the just-in-time system.

HOW *taxes* affect your COMPANY

There's an old saying in business: "Don't let your tax tail wag your investment dog." In other words, taxes should never be the primary reason you make strategic business decisions.

That's not to say that taxes don't belong in your company's overall decision-making calculus. They do. Any expense that can lop off 40 percent—or more—of your company's earnings should not be overlooked.

Depending on what kind of business yours is, it must consider the potential effects of a combination of four taxes: income taxes, self-employment taxes, employment taxes, and excise taxes.

Income Taxes

How much your company owes in income taxes is not simply based on how much profit it generates. The type of company it is and who its owners are matter, too.

If you work for a corporation, your company pays corporate taxes based on the income it generates. The rates are slightly different than individual income tax rates, but they work much the same. In addition, corporate investors are taxed on their share of the company's profits through dividends.

But not all businesses are corporations. Some businesses, such as sole proprietorships and partnerships, aren't required to file income tax returns at all. Rather, the owners of the company are taxed on the company's profits based on their individual income tax brackets.

Pay as You Go

Whether a company's owners pay income taxes on their share of the business's profits or the company pays corporate taxes, the system works on a pay-as-you-go basis. That means your company must deposit a portion of its tax bill with the IRS every quarter throughout the year. These are called *estimated tax payments*. They are called that because it is impossible to determine with accuracy how much taxable income your company will generate over the course of a year. So it pays an estimated bill. Any discrepancy between what your company eventually owes and what it paid is resolved at the end of the tax year.

Those of you who are self-employed understand how this system works. Under pay-as-you-go, self-employed workers send in estimated tax payments to the IRS for their individual income taxes since, unlike salaried employees, they have no company that periodically withdraws taxes from their paychecks.

This may sound like an insignificant point, but quarterly estimated taxes are a critical consideration—or at least they ought to be—as your company assembles its cash budget and manages its cash flow. Imagine what would happen if your company overlooked these estimated taxes. Let's say you work for Allied Manufacturing Corp. Last year, Allied raked in $18 million in taxable income, after factoring in the deductions and exemptions it was eligible for. In 1997, Allied owed the IRS $6.3 million in income taxes. Divide that by four, and Allied's quarterly estimated tax bill was approximately $1.6 million. For Allied, then, failure to consider estimated income taxes was akin to forgetting to pay 1,000 phone bills.

While we're on the subject of self-employment...

Self-Employment Taxes

Self-employment taxes represent the Social Security and Medicare taxes that individuals who work for themselves owe. All workers pay into the Social Security Administration, which runs the Social Security System, and the Health Care Financing Administration, the federal agency that oversees Medicare. But the contributions of salaried employees are matched by their employers. Since the self-employed have no company to play this role, the IRS expects them to cover both portions.

You may be wondering why a business should concern itself with self-employment taxes. Depending on the type of company yours is, its profits may revert to the owners of the company. In these situations, such as partnerships or sole proprietorships, the owners of the business are technically considered self-employed. So self-employment taxes must be considered along with other business taxes.

WHICH ACCOUNTING METHOD DOES YOUR COMPANY USE?

If your company uses *cash basis* accounting, it must report income in the year it is received. Furthermore, it deducts expenses in the year in which it pays them.

If your company uses *accrual basis* accounting, it reports income in the year it is *earned,* even if it hasn't received payment yet. It also deducts expenses in the year it *incurs* them, even if it has yet to pay them.

Employment Taxes

Employment taxes are broken out into the following three categories:

- *Income taxes.* Here, we're not talking about what your company owes, so much as what its employees do. With every paycheck, your company is responsible for withholding—or subtracting—a portion of its employees' income taxes.

- *Social security and medicare taxes.* As we mentioned before, we all pay into Social Security and Medicare. With each paycheck, your company is

responsible for deducting FICA taxes (FICA stands for the Federal Insurance Contributions Act) to cover the entitlements. It is also responsible for making matching contributions.

- *Federal unemployment taxes.* Under the Federal Unemployment Tax Act, commonly referred to as FUTA, businesses are required to pay into a pool of funds held by the federal and state governments to cover unemployment compensation. Unlike FICA taxes, though, FUTA taxes are only required of companies—not individuals. There are also state unemployment taxes, known as SUTA.

Excise Taxes

Your company may owe excise taxes based on: 1) the products it sells; 2) the business it's in; or 3) the equipment or facilities it uses.

Excise taxes are levied by governments for a number of reasons. Two of the major ones are to raise revenues and, in some cases, to curb behavior that they deem harmful or objectionable. For instance, if your company runs a betting pool, it could be slapped with federal excise taxes on wagering. If so, it would have to fill out IRS Form 730. If your company makes, sells, or imports guns, tobacco, or alcohol products, it may owe a variety of excise taxes. If so, it would have to file forms with the Bureau of Alcohol, Tobacco, and Firearms.

In general, your company must file IRS Form 720 for excise taxes that cover:

- Luxuries

- Fuel

- Environmental concerns

- Communications

- The sale and/or use of trucks

- Manufacturing

What Your Company Owes

If the company is a...	It or the owner may have to pay...
Corporation	• Corporate Tax
	• Income Tax (investors)
	• Employment Tax
	• Excise Tax
Subchapter-S Corporation	• Income Tax (shareholders)
	• Employment Tax
	• Excise Tax
Partnership	• Annual Return of Income
	• Self-Employment Tax
	• Employment Tax
	• Excise Tax
Sole Proprietorship	• Income Tax (owner)
	• Self-Employment Tax
	• Employment Tax
	• Excise Tax

Who Pays What?

To figure out how much tax your company owes, first determine how much *taxable income* it throws off.

Taxable income is a company's gross profits minus an assortment of exemptions and deductions it may qualify for. For instance, interest expenses from a mortgage loan can be deducted from gross income. That means the business can subtract, dollar for dollar, the amount of money it paid for these expenses from its gross income, leaving it with less taxable income.

PROPER FORM

You'll need a scorecard to determine which companies must file which IRS Forms. In general:

- *Sole Proprietors* file Form 1040 Schedule C.

- *Partners* must file Form 1065.

- *Corporations* must file Form 1120.

- *Subchapter-S Corporations* must file Form 1120S.

Next, you must consider what type of company yours is. For tax purposes, there are essentially four different types of business entities: sole proprietorships, partnerships, corporations, and subchapter-S corporations.

Sole Proprietorships

A sole proprietorship is the simplest form of business. It is an unincorporated company owned by a single individual.

According to the IRS, a sole proprietorship cannot exist without its owner.

This means that: 1) all of the earnings of a sole proprietorship belong to the owner; 2) all of the assets belong to the owner; and 3) so, too, do all of the company's liabilities. Should the company be sued, for instance, for negligence, the owner of the sole proprietorship would bear the burden of liability. Should the owner pass away or quit, leaving no heirs, the business would cease to exist.

Many companies start off as sole proprietorships.

Proprietorships are relatively easy to organize and are subject to the least amount of regulation. But sole proprietorships have difficulty raising large amounts of capital. As a result, sole proprietors often turn to partners—or seek incorporation—as they grow.

How Are Sole Proprietorships Taxed?

A sole proprietorship does not pay income taxes. Rather, its income and expenses are filed on the owner's individual returns. The income taxes owed will be based on the individual income tax rate of the owner.

Since the owner of a sole proprietorship is technically self-employed, self-employment taxes must also be a consideration, along with employment taxes and excise taxes—depending on what kind of business it is and what it sells.

Partnerships

A partnership is similar to a sole proprietorship, only that more than one person owns the company. Partnerships are defined as businesses owned by two or more persons, each of whom "contributes money, property, labor, or skill, and expects to share in the profits and losses of the business," says the IRS.

Along with the profits of a company, partners must be willing to share its liabilities. In fact, each partner may be liable for the company's total debts, which makes this a somewhat unattractive business form.

Terms like joint ventures and syndicates often refer to partnerships.

How Are Partnerships Taxed?

Like a sole proprietorship, partnerships are not subject to income taxes. Rather, the partners are

DID YOU KNOW...

...that unlike employees, who receive a W-2 Form from their companies, partners in a partnership get a K-1 Form that details what they earned through business income?

taxed based on the income—or loss—they derive from the partnership. The tax rate is based on the partner's own income tax bracket. In fact, unlike all other businesses, partnerships aren't even required to file an annual income tax return. Instead, partnerships file something called an *annual information return.* This lets the IRS know the names and addresses of each partner, along with his or her share of the taxable income.

The partners in a partnership are required to file IRS Form 1065, which indicates their taxable income based on the company's earnings, by April 15 of the year following that tax year. (The percentage of income or loss that a partner is responsible for ought to be outlined in the general partnership agreement.)

Partners are responsible for paying income taxes and estimated taxes throughout the year. In addition, partners, like sole proprietors, are not employees of a company. Therefore, they are subject to self-employment taxes. Obviously, the company is subject to the applicable employment and excise taxes, too.

OTHER BUSINESSES TAXED AS CORPORATIONS

In addition to legally chartered corporations, the following companies formed before 1997 are also taxed as corporations:

- Joint-stock companies

- Insurance companies

- Any business formed before 1997 that has two of the following characteristics: 1) centralization of management; 2) continuity of life; 3) free transferability of interests; 4) limited liability.

Corporations

A corporation is a legal entity recognized by government as existing apart from its owners. Indeed, corporations have interests apart from their owners.

For instance, unlike partnerships or sole proprietorships, corporations can buy and sell assets in their own names. Corporations can sue to protect their trademarks, patents, and interests. They can also be *sued.*

Corporations adhere to their own bylaws and are governed by a board of directors.

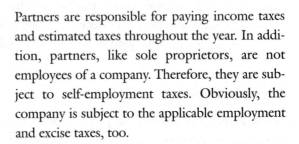

Sample Corporate Tax Rates

If your company generated this much taxable income...	...it pays this much in taxes...	...in addition to this %...	...on the amount over...
$0–$50,000	$0	15	$0
$50,000–$75,000	7,500	25	50,000
$75,000–$100,000	13,750	34	75,000
$100,000–$335,000	22,250	39	100,000
$335,000–$10,000,000	113,900	34	335,000
$10,000,000–$15,000,000	3,400,000	35	10,000,000
$15,000,000–$18,333,333	5,150,000	38	15,000,000
$18,333,333 or more	$0	35	$0

How Are Corporations Taxed?

Because a corporation exists apart from its owners, the company itself can be taxed. In fact, income generated by corporations is said to be taxed *twice:* once, when the company itself pays corporate taxes; and again, when profits generated by the company are distributed to shareholders in the form of dividends. Dividend income is taxed at the shareholder's individual rate. The company is taxed at its own corporate rate.

If you look at the chart above, you'll see what corporate tax rates were in 1997. You'll notice that corporate tax rates, like individual income taxes, depend on the taxable income generated over the course of the year.

Where You Can Get More Information

For more information on:

- *Partnership taxes,* check out **IRS Publication 541.**

- *Corporate taxes,* check out **IRS Publication 542.**

- *Subchapter-S corporations,* check out **Form 1120S** and **Instructions to Form 1120S.**

- *Small business taxes,* check out **IRS Publication 334: Tax Guide for Small Business.**

You can log onto the IRS Web site at http://www.irs.treas.gov to download the forms.

The corporation is also subject to estimated taxes, employment taxes, and possibly excise taxes.

Subchapter-S Corporations

What is a Subchapter-S corporation? It is a small corporation—with 75 or fewer shareholders—that qualifies for a provision found in section S of the IRS code. This section gives small corporations the *option* of operating as a corporation, while being taxed as a partnership.

Why would a company want to do this? For starters, it avoids double taxation.

The company itself does not owe taxes. Like a partnership, the Subchapter-S owners split the profits and are taxed at their own rates. By remaining a corporation, though, the shareholders are protected in terms of liability.

How Are Subchapter-S Corporations Taxed?

As we've noted, a Subchapter-S does not pay corporate taxes. Its taxable income is passed through to the company's shareholders. The company is subject, however, to estimated taxes, employment taxes, and possibly excise taxes.

NEVER HEARD OF A SUBCHAPTER-S?

Perhaps you've heard it called something else, such as a:

- Tax-option corporation

- Small business corporation

BORROWING *money* and *raising* CAPITAL

CHAPTER THIRTEEN

We've been programmed to believe that borrowing money—and debt in general—is a bad thing. But what if you knew you could borrow money at, say, 2 percent and turn around and invest it at a 5 percent rate of return?

You'd borrow it, right? Of course you would. That's because there are strategic reasons to seek financing.

Leverage

Let's say you've just discovered the next Microsoft—the next hot growth stock. Unfortunately, you don't have any cash to invest. So, you go to the bank and take out a loan for $50,000. You take that money and buy 5,000 shares of this company's stock at $10 a share. A month goes by and the stock is trading at $15 a share. A year goes by, and it's up to $50 a share. Your original investment of $50,000 is now worth $250,000.

But wait. You didn't really invest $50,000 of your own money. You invested $50,000 of the bank's money. Assuming that the bank charged you 8 percent interest on the loan, you've actually only spent $4,000 to take out the loan. In effect, what you've done is taken $4,000 and turned it into $200,000 ($250,000 minus the original $50,000 cost of the stock)—that's a return of 4,900 percent on your original investment.

This is called *leverage*. In finance, leverage refers to the amount of debt a company carries on its books.

Why Companies Borrow

The leverage—or power—of borrowed capital is one reason why all companies, even the most profitable ones, seek financing from time to time.

For instance, let's say your company wants to build a new distribution center, which will cost $5 million. And let's say your company is sitting on $5 million in cash and marketable securities. So if it wanted to, it could pay for the new facility out of its own accounts. Doing so would seemingly save $1.1 million in interest payments, assuming the alternative would be to take out a five-year, intermediate-term bank loan at 8 percent.

But that would tie up $5 million for five years. What if the company knew it could get a 12 percent return on its investment if it used that $5 million not for its distribution center, but to form a joint venture with a competitor? In that case, that $5 million could generate $3.8 million over five years. In effect, then, the company would *lose* $2.7 million by using its own cash.

Of course, not all companies seek financing for strategic purposes. Others do it because they need cash to expand—or just to stay in business.

FREE MONEY

An account payable, or trade credit, has several advantages. For instance:

- It's usually interest-free.

- It's easy to get.

- It doesn't require collateral.

Issues to Consider When Borrowing

Before it borrows money, your company must consider a variety of issues. For starters, there is a danger in being over-leveraged. At some point, a company can take on too much debt for its own good, and its ability to meet its obligations is compromised. In addition, *when* your company takes on debt can be just as critical as *how much* debt it takes on. Here, then, are some important things to consider:

- *Sales trends.* Will your company be able to repay the loan out of its growing cash flow and earnings?

- *Interest rates.* Are rates favorable now, or should the company wait for more favorable financing conditions later on?

- *Inflation.* If inflation is rising, the company could end up repaying the loan with cheaper dollars. If there's deflation, the loan could be more expensive than the company first assumed.

- *Taxes.* Some interest payments, such as mortgage interest, are tax deductible.

Choices of Financing

The type of financing your company chooses will depend largely on what it needs the money for, how much it needs, how soon it can pay it back, and the terms of the financing it can negotiate. There are four basic types of financing that companies can choose from:

- Short-term credit

- Intermediate-term loans

- Long-term debt

- Equity

LESS IS NOT MORE

It's impossible to know when emergencies may arise. So when it comes to short-term financing, the rule of thumb is that it's better to obtain more than you need, rather than less.

This is especially true with lines of credit, since companies aren't required to use every dollar of credit extended to them, and since the interest rate is relatively low.

TO BE OR NOT TO BE...SECURED

If a loan requires collateral, it is a *secured loan*. If it doesn't, it's *unsecured*. For obvious reasons, businesses prefer to obtain unsecured financing.

While some lenders don't require collateral, they may force borrowers to maintain a *compensating balance,* or minimum balance in their checking accounts. This could be as much as 20 percent of the loan amount. In a sense, then, the compensating balance is cash serving as partial collateral for the loan.

Collateral and compensating balances both make the actual cost of the loan higher, since those assets can't be invested or liquidated during the life of the loan.

Short-Term Financing

Short-term financing represents loans and credit that must be repaid within a year. Companies often require short-term financing to cover basic business operations and to meet current obligations.

For instance, let's assume your company owes $5 million, due on the tenth of the month. Let's further assume that it has enough current assets to cover those obligations. But what if most of its assets are tied up in accounts receivable, which might not be repaid for another month? In the interim, it may decide to rely on short-term credit to pay its bills and stay in business. Once it collects payments on its accounts receivable, it then pays back its lender.

In general, lenders only offer short-term credit to companies that can repay the loan out of *normal cash flow.* That means a company that may have to sell off assets—or even take out additional loans to pay back this one—won't be able to secure this type of credit.

The most desirable form of short-term credit is a *trade credit*—the grace period that a company's suppliers give it to pay for goods and supplies already shipped. Businesses aren't charged interest during the 30 to 60 days it normally takes to pay back trade credits. For many companies, especially small ones, trade credits could represent as much as half of their total short-term debt.

Line of Credit

A line of credit is negotiated through a bank. There's a maximum line of credit extended to the company, but it is under no obligation to use it all up. Businesses must pay interest only on that portion of money they *actually* borrow. The credit generally remains intact as long as your company's credit circumstances do not change.

Guaranteed Revolving Credit

If circumstances change—for instance, if your business's credit rating is downgraded—a bank has the right to rescind its line of credit, much as a credit card company has the right to cancel a cardholder's account. That's why businesses often negotiate separate credit agreements with banks for *guaranteed revolving credit*. These agreements are more expensive to obtain since the company is not only paying interest on the money it *actually* borrows, but also a commission to the bank—called a commitment fee—based on the total amount of credit the bank provides.

Factoring

In addition to formal lines of bank credit, companies can obtain financing through finance companies, or *factors*. Factoring is a type of short-term financing, backed by accounts receivables, for companies that either don't qualify for bank credit, or whose short-term credit needs are too large to be met solely by traditional lines of credit. Generally, the factor will charge the company 2 to 3 percentage points in interest above the prime rate, which is the rate banks charge to their most creditworthy clients.

OTHER TYPES OF SHORT-TERM FINANCING

- *Commercial Paper*. This is a type of unsecured note that large, creditworthy companies can use. The interest rates tend to be *below* the prime rate.

- *Inventory Financing*. This is a type of secured loan backed by a company's inventory assets. Generally, companies will resort to inventory financing if factoring is no longer a viable option.

WHERE CAN YOU FIND A FACTOR?

The Edwards Directory of American Factors is a list of more than 200 factors throughout the country. It's available at most public libraries. Or, you can call the Edwards Research Group in Newton, MA, at (800) 963-1993.

In a typical factoring arrangement, a company turns over its accounts receivable to a finance company in exchange for 50 to 80 percent of their value. This represents the short-term cash the company needs. In some situations, the company continues to receive payment on those accounts, and then turns over that money to the factor as it rolls in. In other cases, it's the factor who's in charge of collecting the receivables. (This can actually be advantageous to the company, since it would no longer have to serve as or hire a collection agency.)

Once all of the receivables are paid off, the factor returns to the company the remaining 20 percent to 50 percent of the value of the receivables, less the commissions and fees. Sometimes, those can be as high as 5 percent, though typically, they're closer to 2 percent.

Intermediate-Term Loans

Intermediate-term loans are formalized secured loan agreements between businesses and banks that must be repaid in one to five years. They are generally used to purchase fixed assets.

Because companies require this money for a longer period of time than short-term credit, they pay a slightly higher rate of interest for intermediate-term loans. However, the company can pay back the money in installments—each consisting of part interest and part principal—based on an amortization schedule negotiated between the lender and the borrower.

How Costly Are These Loans?

To calculate the cost of a loan, you must first determine if the loan is based on a *simple* or *discounted* interest rate. A bank loan based on *simple interest* is easy to figure

out—it's based on the stated interest rate. Let's say your company takes out a $10 million loan that matures in one year. If the interest rate is 7 percent, your company would have to pay back $10.7 million at the end of the year. In other words, the loan will cost your firm $700,000.

$10,000,000 x 0.07 = $700,000

Now, let's say your company's loan was based on a *discounted interest rate*. This means the lender will deduct the amount of interest from the loan *up front*. Instead of receiving $10 million from the bank, then, your company will only get $9.3 million in financing.

$10,000,000 x 0.07 = $700,000

$10,000,000 – $700,000 = $9,300,000

In this case, the effective cost of the loan is not 7 percent, but rather 7.53 percent. That's because you've effectively prepaid 7 percent interest on a $10 million loan, which is the equivalent of 7.53 percent interest on a $9.3 million loan.

$10,000,000 x 0.07 = $700,000

$700,000/$9.3 million = 0.0753

Long-Term Debt

Though generally used to purchase fixed assets, long-term debt can also support a company's

FACTORING

- *Notification basis factoring.* In this arrangement, when a company's customers purchase products, they pay the factor directly, rather than the company.

- *Non-notification factoring.* This arrangement works like a basic loan. The customers pay the company for products delivered. And then the company pays back the factor based on the receivables collected.

DID YOU KNOW...

...that January 10th is a critical date for many retailers? Often, that's when their payments are due to factors for credits extended prior to the holiday shopping season.

Who Relies on Factoring?

Businesses whose sales and cash flow are concentrated in a single quarter or season tend to rely on factors.

Retailers, for instance, purchase the majority of their annual inventories in the months leading into the fourth quarter of each year. Typically, the cost of this merchandise outstrips their ability to pay, given their cash flow situation. Monies advanced to them by factors are used to pay for the merchandise and to cover immediate obligations.

In fact, reliance on factors is so prevalent in the retail industry that economists gauge how strong or weak holiday shopping seasons are, based on the speed with which retailers pay back obligations to their factors.

ongoing financial needs. Long-term debt comes in a number of forms. For instance, a company can take out:

- *Bank loans.* Banks offer loans maturing in 5 to 15 years with either variable or fixed rates.

- *Mortgages.* In many cases, a company will use a mortgage to help finance new buildings or factories.

- *Bonds.* A bond is a form of long-term debt *sold* by companies to outside investors. The investors, then, take on the role of creditors. Bonds can be used to finance long-term projects.

Bonds

Think of a bond as an IOU. Companies sell these IOUs to raise money, typically for

long-term projects. Each IOU has a date of maturity printed on it, which represents the date on which the company agrees to pay back the investor. In the meantime, investors charge interest on the bond.

There are a variety of different types of bonds your company can issue. They include:

- *Debentures.* Unlike mortgages, debentures are unsecured. This means they are backed not by an asset, but by the full faith and credit of the company. As a result, investors must rely on a company's credit rating to determine the risk associated with a company's bond—and what rate of interest to charge. For instance, companies with poor ratings must offer higher yields on their bonds than companies with high ratings. The bonds of these companies are commonly referred to as *junk,* whereas the bonds of highly rated companies are called *investment grade.*

- *Subordinated debentures.* These IOUs generally offer higher interest rates than straight debentures. That's because, in the event of bankruptcy, the holders of these bonds must wait for other creditors to recoup their money before they can make claims on the company's assets.

- *Convertible bonds.* These types of IOUs give investors the option of converting the IOU into common stock of the company. Because of this feature, convertible bonds often pay lower interest rates.

- *Mortgage-backed bonds.* This is one type of bond that is secured. Your company may finance the construction of new buildings or facilities with these instruments. Should it default, the creditors can simply take possession of the real estate.

BRIDGE FINANCING

Sometimes, a company will arrange for a series of intermediate-term loans. When there are gaps, though, between the time one loan expires and another kicks in, it may need short-term loans to bide its time. These loans are referred to as *bridge financing.*

Bond Ratings

The two leading bond-rating services in the United States are Moody's Investor Service and Standard & Poor's. They rely on slightly different ratings systems:

Moody's	Standard & Poor's	Description
Aaa	AAA	This is the highest rating possible. It means that the issuing company can be trusted to pay back the principal and interest on its loans.
Aa	AA	High quality: The issuing company's ability to repay debts is strong.
A	A	Good quality: The issuing company's ability to repay debts is good.
Baa	BBB	Adequate: This is the lowest rating a company can enjoy while still being called "investment grade."
Ba	BB	Now, companies are entering the category of speculative, or junk bonds.
Caa	B	This indicates poor quality.
Ca	CCC	This rating is very risky.
C	C	This represents the lowest rating.
D	D	The company is in default.

Equity

In addition to selling debt, companies can raise capital by selling shares of ownership in the firm. They can do this while still remaining *private*. For instance, the company's owners can sell a portion of ownership in the business to outside investors through a *private placement*. Or, a company can raise capital through a *public offering*, where its shares are listed on an open stock exchange.

Unlike debt, equity financing does not need to be repaid. Investors willing to buy a stake in a company are speculating that the business will become profitable. And the cash they use to place those bets is the basis of the financing.

Equity comes in one of two forms: *common stock* and *preferred stock*. Common stock owners have a say in how the business is run. However, they are typically last in line when it comes to making claims on the company's assets. For instance, should the business go bankrupt, common stock owners would have to wait for creditors, bond holders and owners of preferred shares to get paid before they are. Owners of *preferred stock* have the opposite problem. While they don't have a say in the management of the company, they are given priority when it comes to receiving dividends and making claims on assets in the event of liquidation.

Going Public

In recent years, an increasing number of firms—perhaps as a result of the decade-long bull market—have elected to go public. That means following an *initial public offer-*

VENTURE CAPITAL

Small, growing companies can turn to *venture capital firms* for long-term financing. Venture capital represents seed money businesses use to get off the ground. While venture capital is technically a loan, companies often repay these funds with shares of equity in the business.

ing, these companies' shares trade on the open market—typically on one of the three major U.S. exchanges: the New York Stock Exchange, the American Stock Exchange, and the Nasdaq National Market.

While public equity offerings represent a fast source of capital, businesses must carefully weigh the pros and cons of this decision. The pros include:

- *Greater liquidity*. Owners of publicly traded companies can easily sell their interests in the firm—or increase them.

- *Additional sources of capital*. The greater the number of investors, the more sources of equity financing there are.

- *A loss of control*. As we noted, common stock owners have a say in how the business is run. They have the right, for instance, to elect the company's board. Also, companies that are public cannot control who owns common stock in the firm.

- *Additional disclosure*. The Securities and Exchange Commission requires public companies to file annual and quarterly reports detailing their income, cash flow, and net worth. Unlike private companies, public companies cannot keep this information from their competitors.

Just because a company "goes public" does not mean it cannot rely on other forms of financing. In fact, in recent years, many public companies have elected to trim their reliance on equity financing by buying back their own stock on the open market.

HOW THE economy affects your company's FINANCES

We all know what happened on October 29, 1929. That was Black Tuesday —the largest single-day drop ever in the U.S. stock market in percentage terms. Investors would lose over $30 billion in the following two weeks, the equivalent of one-third of their wealth.

But why do so many of us care? At the time, only less than 2 percent of Americans invested in stock. The reason has little to do with the effect of the stock market crash and everything to do with what caused it. "The stock market is but a mirror which provides an image of the underlying or fundamental economic situation," the economist John Kenneth Galbraith once said. "Cause and effect run from the economy to the stock market, never the reverse. In 1929, the economy was headed for trouble. Eventually, that trouble was violently reflected in Wall Street."

And eventually, those troubles spilled onto Main Street. As the Great Depression set in, American companies—even those that didn't issue stock—began to realize the significance of the stock market crash: Unemployment would hit a record 25 percent; deflation would set in; and 10,000 banks would suspend operations.

Macroeconomics 101

If the stock market crash of 1929 taught us anything, it was that external forces such as the state of the economy affect a company's income statement and balance sheet—indeed, every company's income statement and balance sheet—just as much as internal decision-making does. That's why your company, when it sits down to create its budgets for the coming year, considers not only its own sales and expense trends, but also those of its industry—and the economy as a whole.

For instance, a retailer in a company town like Detroit must not only worry about its own fortunes, but those of GM, Ford, and Chrysler because the employees of these three companies represent its customers. If the Big Three lay off a quarter of their work forces, the retailer will no doubt feel the effects. That retailer must also consider macroeconomic trends such as:

- *Economic growth.* The faster the economy grows, the more willing and able consumers will be to buy the retailer's merchandise.

- *Inflation.* High inflation can eat away at the purchasing power of that retailer's consumers.

- *Interest rates.* As interest rates rise, it becomes more expensive to borrow money or seek financing. This could affect the retailer's ability to expand.

- *Unemployment.* Consumers without jobs can't afford to buy the retailer's goods.

- *Consumer confidence.* Even if consumers aren't unemployed, if they are insecure about the economy they will be less likely to make purchases.

Economic Growth

Economic growth is the most important indicator of the health of the overall economy. The broadest measure of economic growth is the *Gross Domestic Product*, or *GDP.* Every quarter, the U.S. Commerce Department tallies the total revenues generated by companies and government agencies throughout the country to arrive at GDP.

What makes GDP so useful is that unlike other barometers of economic growth, it is based on actual sales, not projections. In addition, GDP measures economic output based on its actual worth—in dollar amounts—as opposed to the number of goods sold. In fact, the Commerce Department reports economic output in two ways: 1) based on inflation-adjusted dollars, known as *real GDP*; and 2) based on current dollars, or *nominal GDP*.

If real GDP *falls* for more than two consecutive quarters, the economy is said to be in recession. If GDP rises, but less than 2 percent a year, the economy is said to be growing *slowly*. Annual GDP growth of 2–3 percent is considered healthy; above 4 percent is considered robust; and above 5 percent is exceptional.

Ironically, many believe an economy growing 5 percent or more is expanding too quickly. That's because economic growth signals consumption; consumption signals demand; and increased demand tends to lead to inflation.

GDP's Domino Effect

Does GDP give rise to inflation, or does inflation give rise to GDP? It's difficult to say. It's like asking which came first: the chicken or the egg? But whether GDP came first or not, it still has an effect on all other economic indicators. It's useful to see just how in the following simplistic scenarios.

Scenario 1: Strong Growth

Imagine that the Gross Domestic Product rises 4 percent this year. That's a sign of robust economic growth. But an economy that grows too fast

WHAT GDP DOES NOT COUNT

Up until 1991, GDP was referred to as GNP, or Gross National Product. Unlike GNP, GDP does not count net exports—the value of the investments and purchases U.S. companies make overseas minus the investments and purchases that foreign companies make here.

In addition, GDP fails to count the amount of investments Americans make in stocks and bonds. Nor does it tally business transactions that aren't reported to the IRS, such as the sale of illegal drugs and even some nanny services.

leads to inflation. Or so economists believe. So the Federal Reserve decides to do something about it. The most effective way for the Fed to fight inflation is to raise interest rates.

Here's why: By raising rates (the amount the Fed charges *banks* to borrow money), the Fed makes it more expensive for companies to borrow money and obtain financing. Companies that can't afford to borrow money can't build new factories, buy new machinery, or expand. If enough companies are prohibited from expanding, economic expansion will slow, which in turn will stop the threat of inflation. But high interest rates have another effect: They drive up the yield of bonds, another form of financing. And bond yields have an effect on the stock market.

Here's why: The stock and bond markets are interrelated in that investors scour both in hopes of finding the best returns. Bonds are generally less risky than stocks, but bonds often yield only half as much as stocks, which, since 1926, have returned on average, about 10.7 percent a year. As bond yields rise, bonds become more attractive to investors. Investors who sell stocks to buy bonds drive down the stock market.

If stocks fall enough—and for a long enough period of time, such as during the depression in 1929 and the bear market of 1973–1974—it affects the average income of individuals, the tax receipts of governments, the ability of companies to raise financing in the stock market, and consumer confidence. All of these trends hurt spending and economic output, which hurts GDP growth for the following year.

Scenario 2: Slow Growth

This time, let's assume that the Gross Domestic Product is flat, or that it has actually fallen a bit. Perhaps a recession has set in. In this case, the Fed isn't so much concerned about inflation, but rather all of the effects of a recessionary economy. What can the Fed do about this? It can try to spur economic growth. It does this by lowering interest rates. Lower rates encourage companies to spend, since it does not cost as much to borrow money. Lower rates also encourage consumers to buy, since credit card rates, mortgage interest, and car loans will be cheaper.

The Problem with GDP

While Gross Domestic Product measures economic output, it isn't an entirely accurate gauge
of economic progress. That's because GDP
does not distinguish between *positive* and *negative* output.

Consider the effect of a factory that sits on the
banks of a river. Let's say that by day, this factory manufactures
machine parts, generating $10 million of economic output. By night, it
discharges pollutants into the river, which will cost $10 million to clean
up. In fact, let's assume that the local government is forced to hire a
company to do just that.

A reasonable person may conclude that this factory produced $0 in
output, since it sold $10 million in goods, but caused $10 million in
damage.

However, the Commerce Department does not see it this way. In fact,
according to the Commerce Department's measure of GDP, this factory, in effect, added $20 million to GDP. That's because GDP is sim-
ply a blanket measure of goods sold and services rendered. It does
not discriminate between products and services that add to the economic health of the nation and those that detract from it. For instance,
the sale of cigarettes will be counted in GDP, as will the healthcare
costs associated with cigarette use.

Natural disasters, which destroy billions of dollars' worth of assets,
are also a source of economic output, according to GDP. When the
next hurricane strikes Florida, wiping out billions of dollars in homes,
businesses, and personal property, GDP will not count the loss in
assets. It will, however, count the output that is created when construction companies are brought in to rebuild those properties and
when consumers go shopping to replace all the goods they lost.

Lower rates also drive down bond yields, which are the interest rates that governments and corporations agree to pay investors who are willing to lend them money. As bonds become less attractive, investors again look to the stock market as an alternative. As investors buy stocks, stock prices rise. And so, too, does the market as a whole.

In theory, all of this activity leads to enough economic activity to boost GDP.

Other Ways to Measure Economic Growth

Industrial Production

The Industrial Production index, maintained by the Federal Reserve, measures the actual physical output of goods by the nation's factories. It is a much narrower measure of economic growth, since it excludes a number of things that contribute to GDP, such as government spending, agriculture, and the service sector. But unlike GDP figures, which are released quarterly, industrial production figures are announced monthly, making it a more timely measure.

Durable Goods

Durable goods are big-ticket items with lifespans of at least three years which are generally purchased by businesses. An engine, for instance, purchased by a carmaker would be considered a durable good. By adding up the orders that factories receive each month for these goods, economists learn whether businesses and/or individuals are confident enough about the economy to invest large amounts of money at a given moment.

Capacity Utilization

Each month, the Federal Reserve determines how busy factories are. It does this by determining what the overall capacity of U.S. factories is, and then calculating at what percent of that capacity factories have been operating. If the nation's factories can make 1 million refrigerators a month, for instance, but produce only 500,000, it's a sign that the economy may be slowing.

Business Startups and Bankruptcies

Each year, thousands of new businesses open up, and thousands more close for good. The more companies that are established, and the fewer established companies that close, the better the economy is. Or so many economists believe.

Luckily, you don't have to pour over thousands of bankruptcy records and business permits to find out this information. Dun & Bradstreet, the New York City-based credit company, publishes these numbers annually.

Other Measures of Economic Health

Consumer Confidence

John Kenneth Galbraith noted that the role of the individual in the economy is not to save or invest, "but to consume its products." Individuals, however, tend not to consume during periods of economic uncertainty. After all, you wouldn't buy a car if you were afraid that you might be laid off in the next six months, right?

Routinely, the Conference Board takes a poll of the level of optimism that consumers have in the economy. The University of Michigan and other institutions conduct similar surveys. Though it is difficult to say how accurate these studies are in predicting consumer behavior, these measures do give businesses a general idea of how willing consumers may be to make purchases in the coming year.

These surveys are particularly useful when their results diverge from GDP trends. For instance, when the economy was growing at 3 percent in 1992–1993, consumer confidence surveys indicated that Americans were still insecure enough

INDEX OF LEADING ECONOMIC INDICATORS

Because no one thing—not GDP, not inflation, not interest rates—tell the whole picture of the health of the economy, some businesses turn to the so-called Index of Leading Economic Indicators to gauge the health of the economy. The index, which is published in the *Wall Street Journal*, consists of about a dozen economic indicators, including the stock market, unemployment, and inventory fluctuations.

about the economy not to spend in a manner reflective of overall economic growth. In fact consumer confidence was as low then as it was during the recession of 1981–1982. It's not surprising why. During this period of time, many of the largest American companies, such as AT&T, GM, and IBM were "downsizing" their work-forces.

HOW TO CAPITALIZE ON UNEMPLOYMENT

When unemployment is on the rise, consider *increasing* your work force, rather than downsizing—so long as your company can afford to expand during these periods.

Why? The rules of supply and demand say that when there are more workers looking for jobs than there are jobs for them, employers can dictate wages. Experienced engineers, for instance, who may have commanded salaries in excess of $100,000 a year, may be willing to work at your company for just $75,000 during periods of high unemployment.

Unemployment

Each month, the Labor Department counts the number of Americans who are unemployed. Obviously, individuals who don't have jobs can't afford to spend. So high unemployment can have a real impact on consumption. It can also have an impact on overall consumer confidence.

Bear in mind that it's impossible to reach full employment, or an unemployment rate of 0 percent, since some people don't need to work; others can't; and still others choose to stay home and tend to their homes. In fact, some degree of unemployment is desirable, since economists believe that low unemployment—like robust economic growth—can lead to inflation.

Economists tend to think an unemployment rate of about 5 percent is ideal. This means that 19 of every 20 Americans who are actively seeking jobs find one. It was only as recently as 1997 that the government was able to bring unemployment down to this level. In 1981, during the height of the last recession, unemployment stood at 10 percent, which means that for every ten Americans who wanted to work, one could not find a job.

Inflation

Inflation measures the routine rise in prices of goods and services. The laws of supply and demand say that prices will rise when: 1) the cost of manufacturing goods increases; 2) products are so popular that demand outstrips supply; or 3) the economy is so flush with cash that consumers go searching for goods and services to buy. During economic booms, when spending is on the rise, economists tend to fear the rise of inflation.

Inflation is measured in several ways. But the most popular way is the *Consumer Price Index*, or *CPI*. Periodically the Bureau of Labor Statistics prices a basket of around 100,000 goods that supposedly represent a cross-section of consumer spending. The basket includes the cost of groceries, housing, transportation, clothing, and entertainment.

If the basket of goods costs 5 percent more to purchase this year than last year, inflation is said to be growing at rate of 5 percent. If the basket of goods costs the same this year compared to last, inflation is nonexistent. And if prices actually *fall* from one period to another, inflation gives way to *deflation*.

Inflation has grown, on an annualized basis, about 3–4 percent a year for the past century. Annual inflation of 2 percent or less is considered optimal; 3 percent is acceptable; 4 percent is cause for concern; and 5 percent or more is considered extremely serious.

MAKING INFLATION WORK FOR YOU

Depending on your perspective, inflation can be a good thing. Remember back in 1981, when the country was going through *hyperinflation?* Double-digit inflation jacked up our gas prices, car prices, clothing, and grocery bills. But it also increased the price of houses, making home ownership a worthwhile investment.

In fact, during inflationary times, some believe it's best to hold tangible assets such as real estate and gold since they tend to *appreciate* in value, rather than depreciate. However, this strategy does not always work. Consider the price of gold, which over the past two decades has lost two-thirds of its value.

Why Should We Care?

You may not be overly concerned about inflation these days, since it was growing less than 3 percent a year in 1997. But we should all worry about inflation because it eats away at our purchasing power.

For instance, let's say you're 35 years old and have managed to save $20,000. You're fearful of the stock market and distrustful of banks, so you stick that $20,000 in a safety deposit box. Thirty years pass and finally you decide to spend the money. Unfortunately, that $20,000 is no longer worth $20,000. Assuming a 4 percent rate of inflation—which compounds annually—that $20,000 now has the purchasing power of less than $6,200.

THE PRODUCER PRICE INDEX

Another way to measure inflation is through the Producer Price Index.

Unlike CPI, the PPI measures changes in the price of goods sold to businesses, including raw materials, such as steel and wood; semi-finished products, such as sheet metal and timber; and finished products, such as cars and office equipment.

Inflation has a similar effect on companies. As we discussed in chapter 9, businesses set aside cash for strategic purposes, such as acquisitions or investments in other companies. Let's say your firm has set aside $1 million for strategic acquisitions. Should inflation rise 7 percent a year, for just five years, that $1 million would be worth around $300,000 less.

Inflation also wreaks havoc on inventory management. Let's say your firm maintains an inventory of goods at the beginning of the year valued at $10 million that turns over multiple times a year. If inflation were soaring into the double digits, as it was in 1981, by the end of the year that inventory would be worth as much as $11.2 million and the company would have to raise prices to cover the cost of goods sold. (So replacing all that inventory at the beginning of the year may cost $10 million, but because of inflation, replacing it again at the end of the year could cost $11.2 million.)

Consumer Price Index

Year	All Items
1997	1.7
1996	3.3
1995	2.5
1994	2.6
1993	3.0
1992	3.0
1991	4.2
1990	5.4
1989	4.8
1988	4.1
1987	3.7
1986	1.9
1985	3.6
1984	4.4
1983	3.2
1982	6.2
1981	10.4
1980	13.5

From an investor's standpoint, perhaps the greatest threat inflation poses is regarding wages. Just as the federal government increases Social Security payments to retirees based on CPI adjustments, many companies have negotiated contracts with workers to offer cost-of-living raises tied to the CPI. That means if they budgeted $5 million in wages payable this year, and inflation ticks up 10 percent, they'd have to find another $500,000 somewhere to cover their expenses. This is why Wall Street considers wage inflation one of the primary threats to corporate earnings.

Interest Rates

Interest rates are the premiums that lenders charge to borrowers for loans. They are the rates at which companies buy additional equipment, finance the construction of factories, and even invest.

While they are negotiated between lenders and borrowers, the Federal Reserve has the ability to influence rates. That's because the Fed itself is a lender—it lends money on a short-term basis to commercial banks. When it does so, the interest rate *it* charges is known as the *discount rate*. When the Fed raises the discount rate, it forces commercial banks to turn around and charge an even higher rate to their customers. After all, commercial rates will have to be higher than the discount rate for banks to make money.

Why Should We Care?

Borrowing money is a cost of doing business. So rising interest rates tend to put pressure on a company's profits.

Interest rates also help companies decide when to expand and when to put off capital expenditures. For instance, say your company wants to build a new factory as part of a major expansion. How does it know when to build? Certainly, market conditions must be taken into account. But interest rates ought to be factored in, as well.

If the company plans to build the factory two years from now, but sees that interest rates, currently at 5 percent, are headed up, it may make sense to speed up the expansion. After all, borrowing $10 million today at 5 percent will cost your firm $11.3

million, assuming the company pays back the money within five years. Borrowing $10 million two years from now at 10 percent will cost about $1.4 million more—or $12.7 million.

The Bond Market

As we've noted, bonds are IOUs that companies and governments sell to investors to raise money. So, like interest rates, the bond market reflects the cost of raising capital at a given moment in time. To gauge the market, you must keep track of several different types of bonds. They include:

- U.S. Treasuries

- Mortgage-backed Securities

- Investment-grade Corporate Bonds

- Junk Bonds

The Lehman Brothers Aggregate Bond Index is a useful tool to gauge the rise and fall of bond prices and yields.

The Stock Market

The most common measure of the U.S. stock market is the *Dow Jones Industrial Average*, or "The Dow" as most of us refer to it. The list was created in 1884 by Charles Dow, one of the founders of the Dow Jones Co., which publishes *The Wall Street Journal*. Originally, the list was made up of 11 companies whose fortunes Dow believed most accurately reflected the health of the economy. The list was later expanded to 30 stocks.

Can 30 companies adequately gauge trends in the overall economy? Probably not. That's why businesses and investors rely on other stock market indices, such as the *Standard &*

THREE THINGS YOUR COMPANY SHOULD DO WHEN INTEREST RATES ARE RISING

- Hold off making long-term equipment purchases.

- Collect your bills sooner.

- Pay your bills later.

Poor's 500 Stock Index. The S&P 500 is a much broader index that incorporates many of today's fastest-growing companies, such as Microsoft and Intel. The *Nasdaq Composite Index,* which is heavily influenced by technology shares, is another useful gauge of the stock market.

Unlike other indicators of economic health, the stock market offers a daily snapshot of what investors are thinking. The Dow, S&P, and Nasdaq indices not only reflect investor sentiment toward individual companies, but also investor confidence in the health of the economy, economic growth, inflation, interest rates, corporate earnings, and consumer confidence.

Still, it is dangerous to draw any conclusions from a single day of activity in the stock market. For instance, on October 27, 1997, the Dow fell a record 554 points and lost roughly 8 percent of its value. Does that mean the economy was 8 percent less healthy than it was on October 26th? Of course not. But the loss did hint at investor anxiety. The very next day, the Dow *rallied* 302 points, which set a record for the largest single-day gain in the stock market.

TWO THINGS YOUR COMPANY SHOULD DO WHEN INTEREST RATES ARE FALLING

- Invest in heavy machinery and equipment.

- Consider refinancing current loan agreements with lenders.

Sometimes, it takes a year before stock market trends become clear. For example, stocks were mostly flat in 1990 and 1994—when the GDP was flat. They advanced 7–10 percent in 1993 and 1995—when GDP growth was modest. And they advanced more than 20 percent each year from 1995 to 1997, when the economy was robust. Since 1926, stocks have returned an average of roughly 10.7 percent a year.

Why Should We Care?

About 10,000 companies obtain financing in the equity market through the three main exchanges: the New York Stock Exchange, the American Stock Exchange, and the Nasdaq National Market. The fortunes of publicly traded compa-

The Dow Stocks

Who decides which stocks are in the Dow Jones Industrial Average? The editors of *The Wall Street Journal*. Periodically, the editors will take companies off the list and add others onto it. For instance, in 1997, the *Journal's* editors removed Bethlehem Steel, Texaco, Westinghouse, and Woolworth from the list and replaced them with faster-growing Hewlett-Packard, Johnson & Johnson, Travelers, and Wal-Mart.

Still, many complain that the index remains weighted toward old-fashioned industrial manufacturing firms and does not reflect the growing influence of technology in the economy.

Here are the 30 companies that supposedly reflect the health of the economy:

- *Alcoa:* an aluminum manufacturer

- *Allied Signal:* a diversified manufacturer

- *American Express:* the financial services company

- *AT&T:* the nation's largest telecommunications company

- *Boeing:* the world's largest airplane maker

- *Caterpillar:* the world's largest maker of earth-moving equipment

- *Chevron:* the diversified oil company

- *Coca-Cola:* the world's largest beverage company

- *Disney:* the entertainment company

- *DuPont:* the chemical company

- *Eastman Kodak:* makers of cameras, film, and imaging systems

(continued)

(The Dow Stocks, continued)

- *Exxon:* the oil company

- *General Electric:* the diversified manufacturing, media, consumer goods, and financing firm

- *General Motors:* the world's largest automaker

- *Goodyear:* rubber and tire company

- *Hewlett-Packard:* computer and networking company

- *IBM:* computers and information technology firm

- *International Paper:* paper and forest products company

- *Johnson & Johnson:* the diversified medical products company

- *McDonald's:* the largest fast-food chain

- *Merck:* the nation's largest pharmaceutical company

- *Minnesota Mining & Manufacturing:* diversified manufacturer of consumer products

- *J.P. Morgan:* financial services company

- *Philip Morris:* tobacco and food company

- *Procter & Gamble:* the world's largest personal-care products maker

- *Sears:* the nation's second-largest retailer

- *Travelers:* diversified financial services firm

- *Union Carbide:* chemicals company

- *United Technologies:* a diversified manufacturer

- *Wal-Mart:* the world's largest retailer

The Bulls and the Bears

When the stock market rises for a sustained period of time—at least two to three quarters and by 20 to 30 percent—market watchers refer to it as a *bull market*. When stock prices fall for a prolonged period of time—at least two to three quarters—they refer to it as a *bear market*. Why?

It depends on whom you ask. Some think the terms bull and bear refer to the ways both animals attack. For instance, when bulls go after their victims, they put their heads down and lift their horns *upward*. On the other hand, bears attack their prey by slashing with their paws in a *downward* motion. Another explanation is that bulls are known for charging, whereas bears are known for hibernating.

Sometimes, it's unclear when a bull market is actually taken over by the bears. For instance, U.S. stocks have been in a bull market since at least 1987. But stocks lost money in 1990 and were flat in 1994. Weren't those bear markets?

Technically, stocks in those years went through a *correction*, rather than a bear market. A correction is a term for a slight retreat of stock prices—often less than a 10 percent drop—for a short period of time.

The last great bear markets that U.S. investors experienced were during: the recession of 1981–1982, when stocks fell 23 percent; the recession of 1973–1974, when stocks fell 45 percent; and the depression of 1929, when stocks by 1933 had lost almost 89 percent of their value.

nies, obviously, are intimately tied to the stock market. The stock market, though, is a barometer of more than just a single company, as the crash of 1929 demonstrated. Investors in the market consider economic growth, interest rates, inflation, the bond market, consumer confidence, and unemployment.

How the stock market is behaving often helps companies determine where and when to seek financing. During bull markets, when stocks are climbing, a company may decide to take advantage of investor optimism by immediately selling shares in the business. During bear markets, when stocks are retreating, that same company may decide to remain private and find alternative sources of capital. This is why companies pondering an initial public offering hire financial firms to advise them, based on their economic forecasts, on when to launch an IPO.

GLOSSARY

accelerated depreciation: A method of calculating an asset's loss of value that takes into consideration the fact that many assets lose the majority of their value in the first few years rather than consistently over time.

accounting: A set function of businesses that records transactions, assets, and liabilities.

accounts payable: Money owed to creditors for services or goods already received.

accounts payable deferral period: The amount of time it takes a company to pay its bills calculated by dividing its accounts payable by the cost of goods sold per day.

accounts receivable: Payments due a company for goods sold.

accrual basis accounting: A method of accounting that recognizes a transaction when products or services are shipped or received.

accrued current liabilities: Certain obligations not yet due which the company must meet within the next year.

accrued taxes payable: Money the company owes in taxes but is not yet due.

ACH (automated clearinghouse network): A computerized network that facilitates the electronic transfer of checks from one bank to another.

age of inventory ratio: A measurement of the speed with which a company is selling its goods. It is calculated by dividing the inventory turnover ratio into 365 days.

aging schedule: A table that indicates the number of days accounts receivable have been outstanding.

annual report: A financial document prepared once a year that includes the balance sheet, income statement, and statement of cash flows.

appreciate: To increase in value over a period of time.

asset: Something of value that can be used to serve a company's needs. Examples of assets are cash, stocks, bonds, inventories, buildings, factories, and goodwill. [See: current assets and fixed assets.]

audit: A professional examination of a company's financial records to gauge the accuracy, appropriateness, and consistency of its accounting practices—and to verify compliance with generally accepted accounting principles.

balance sheet: A document that shows a company's net worth by detailing its assets, liabilities, and owners' equity at a given moment in time.

bankruptcy: The legal process by which corporations or individuals legally announce that they are unable to pay their debts—and which attempts to satisfy creditors' claims.

bear market: An extended period of falling stock prices.

bond: An instrument of debt that pays interest to its holders and that enables a company or government to raise money.

book value: A measurement of a company's net worth, or shareholder equity.

bottom line: The figure on an income statement that indicates the net income or net loss, usually after taxes. [See: profit.]

break even: The volume of sales necessary to cover fixed and variable costs.

bridge financing: A short-term loan taken out between the time one intermediate-term loan expires and the next one starts.

budget: A company's revenue and expenditure plan.

bull market: An extended period of rising stock prices.

business plan: A planning document that outlines how a company intends to allocate its resources, the products it intends to sell, how many units of each product it will make, how it will price the products, how it will market them, and how it will control costs.

capacity utilization: A measure of economic activity calculated by the Federal Reserve which compares the utilization of U.S. factories in relation to their overall capacity.

capital budget: A plan for financing long-term expenditures, such as the construction of new facilities.

carrying costs: The variable expenses associated with ordering inventory—such as the costs of capital, storage, handling, taxes, and insurance—that rise and fall depending on the size of the order.

cash basis accounting: A method of accounting that recognizes a sale when payment is received and recognizes expenses when payment is sent.

cash flow: The movement of cash into and out of a company's accounts during a specific period of time that alters the company's accounts.

cash flow statement: A financial document that indicates how cash has flowed into and out of a company's accounts during a specific period of time.

cash management: The process by which a company determines how much money it needs and maintains just to cover liabilities, investing the remainder at the highest possible rates for the longest possible periods.

CEO (chief executive officer): The head of a corporation.

certificate of deposit: A bank investment that allows a company to receive a fixed rate of return on the principal.

CFO (chief financial officer): A manager whose function is to oversee the finances of a company.

check-clearing float: The time it takes for the Federal Reserve processing center or local clearing-house to make funds available for use after receiving a check.

collateral: Assets used to secure an obligation.

collection float: The time it takes for checks mailed by a company's customers to be accessible by the firm, calculated by adding mail float, processing float, and check-clearing float.

common stock: A type of stock that entitles the holder to voting rights in the issuing company. If a corporation goes out of business, holders of common stock are paid last after creditors, bond holders, and preferred stockholders.

compensating balance: The minimum balance maintained in an account that serves as partial collateral for a bank loan or credit.

consumer confidence: A measure of the optimism that the general public has in the economy.

controller: The chief accountant of a company whose responsibility is to assess performance, account for assets and liabilities, and plan.

convertible bond: A long-term debt instrument that gives the investor the option of converting it into equity, usually common stock.

corporate bond: A debt instrument issued by corporations to raise money.

corporation: A legal business entity that exists separate from its owners.

correction: A slight retreat of stock prices—often less than a 10 percent drop—over a short period of time.

cost of capital: The opportunity costs of the money invested in the company.

CPI (consumer price index): A measure of inflation based on the changes in price of a basket of representative goods and services calculated by the Bureau of Labor Statistics.

credit: 1) A decrease in assets or an increase in liabilities and net worth recorded on the right side of a T-account. 2) The ability of a company or individual to borrow money—or the actual amount of money borrowed.

current assets: Assets that are intended to be liquidated in the normal course of business, usually within a year. Examples of current assets are inventories and accounts receivable.

current cash-to-debt ratio: A figure calculated by dividing a company's operating cash flow by its average current liabilities which indicates its ability to pay bills over time, rather than at a moment in time at the beginning or end of the year.

current cost valuation: A method of valuing assets based on their present worth.

current liability: A short-term obligation that must be met in less than a year.

current ratio: A measurement of a company's ability to pay its short-term debts calculated by dividing current assets by current liabilities.

days payable ratio: A measurement of how quickly a company is paying its vendors.

debenture: An unsecured bond, backed not by an asset, but by the full faith and credit of the issuing company.

debit: An increase in assets or a decrease in liabilities and net worth recorded on the left side of a T-account.

debt: Money owed.

debt ratio: A measurement of a company's liabilities calculated by comparing total liabilities and total assets.

debt-to-equity ratio: A measurement of risk and leverage calculated by dividing total liabilities by shareholder equity.

deflation: The decline in the cost of goods and services.

depository transfer check: An unsigned check that authorizes payment from a local bank to a company's central account without requiring an executive's signature.

depreciate: To decrease in value over a period of time.

direct costs: Expenses companies incur that relate to a specific function in the making and distribution of their products.

disbursement float: The time it takes for a company to mail its payments, and for those payments to be available for use by the firm's creditors.

discounted interest: Interest that is deducted from the amount of a loan up front.

discount rate: The interest rate charged by the Federal Reserve when it lends money to commercial banks.

dividend: A portion of the profits of a corporation paid to its stockholders.

double-entry accounting: A self-balancing system that shows how all transactions consist of an exchange of one thing for another. It records these exchanges as debits and credits to specific accounts.

Dow Jones Averages: A price-weighted average of 30 widely held stocks that serves as a proxy for the performance of the U.S. stock market.

durable goods: Expensive items with lifespans of at least three years.

earnings: [See: profit.]

EOQ (economic ordering quantity) model: A mathematical formula that determines the optimal units of inventory that should be purchased per order, based on ordering costs, carrying costs, and the number units of inventory the company sells per year.

equity: Ownership interest by shareholders in a corporation—in the form of common and preferred stock.

estimated taxes: Taxes prepaid to the IRS every quarter throughout the year based on an estimate of what will be owed.

excise taxes: Taxes levied by the IRS to raise revenues—generally, but not exclusively, on luxury items.

exit cost valuation: A method of valuing assets based on the current liquidation price.

factoring: A type of short-term financing, backed by accounts receivable, for companies that don't qualify for bank credit.

FASB (Financial Accounting Standards Board): The body that governs the accounting profession.

Federal Reserve Bank: One of 12 regional banks and their branches that make up the Federal Reserve System. [See: Federal Reserve System.]

Federal Reserve Board: Seven presidential appointees who make up the governing body of the Federal Reserve System. [See: Federal Reserve System.]

Federal Reserve System: The organization that regulates the U.S. banking and monetary system. [See: Federal Reserve Bank.]

FIFO (First In/First Out): A method of valuing inventory that assumes that the first product manufactured is the first product sold. [See: LIFO.]

financial accounting: The process of gathering financial data and compiling a company's balance sheet, income statement, and cash flow statement.

financial budgets: Budgets such as cash and capital budgets that reflect information found on balance sheets, which detail the financial health of a company at a specific point in time.

financial ratios: Tools based on information in income statements and balance sheets that gauge a company's relative performance in terms of profitability, liquidity, and risk.

finished goods: The products made from raw materials that companies sell.

fixed assets: Assets that will not be liquidated in the normal course of business. Examples of fixed assets can be buildings and factories. But intangibles such as patents, copyrights, and goodwill are also fixed assets.

fixed costs: Expenses that remain constant regardless of sales volume.

flexible budget: A projection for expenses that varies according to sales volume.

float: The time it takes a party to access money after another party has sent payments.

free cash: The amount of cash a company has on hand after capital expenditures are subtracted from operating cash.

GAAP (generally accepted accounting principles): A collection of rules and guidelines for accounting professionals.

G&A (general & administrative) budget: A method of calculating expenses that includes insurance costs, depreciation, support-staff salaries, and licenses and fees.

GDP (gross domestic product): A broad measure of economic activity calculated by the U.S. Commerce Department arrived at by tallying the total dollar value of all goods and services produced in the country over a specific quarter or year.

Great Depression: A period of economic decline during the 1930s triggered by the stock market crash of October 29, 1929.

gross income: The item on an income statement calculated by subtracting the cost of goods sold from net sales.

gross margin: A ratio—calculated by dividing gross income by net sales—that measures a compa-

ny's profit margin on the goods it sells after direct costs have been subtracted.

Health Care Financing Administration: The federal agency that oversees Medicare.

historic cost valuation: A method of measuring an asset at its original cost.

income statement: A document that summarizes a company's revenues, expenses, and profit over a specific period of time.

indirect costs: The item on an income statement that represents expenses that aren't specifically attributable to the acquisition, production, and distribution of products. Examples of indirect costs are bonuses, business travel, and consulting fees.

industrial production index: A measure of economic activity calculated by the Federal Reserve, arrived at by measuring the total physical output of U.S. factories and mines.

inflation: The increase in costs of goods and services.

interest: Payment to a creditor for borrowed money.

interest expense: Expenses incurred as a result of borrowing money.

interest income: Income derived from investing cash in bank accounts, money-market funds, bonds, and so on.

intermediate-term loans: Formalized loan agreements between businesses and banks that must be repaid in one to five years, typically in installments that consist of part interest and part principal.

internal rate of return: A method of determining whether a project should be accepted in a capital budget. IRR represents the rate of return at which the present value of a project's anticipated cash flow equals the present value of its expected costs. In other words, what you will reap from the investment down the line is going to be equal to or greater than what you put into that investment, given that it could have been earning interest elsewhere?

inventory: Raw materials, work in progress, and finished goods intended for sale.

inventory financing: A secured loan backed by a company's inventory assets.

inventory turnover: A measurement of how often a company's inventory is sold and replaced during a specific accounting period. It is calculated by dividing the cost of goods sold by average inventory.

investment-grade bond: A debt instrument issued by a company with a high credit rating.

IPO (initial public offering): A first-time sale of stock to the general public.

junk bond: A high-yielding debt instrument issued by a company with a poor credit rating.

just-in-time (JIT): A sophisticated and expensive method of managing inventory in real time that factors in the speed at which a company manufactures and sells goods.

ledgers: Individual accounts that track a company's liabilities, assets, and net worth.

Lehman Brothers Aggregate Bond Index: An index of bonds that serves as a measurement of bond market performance.

leverage: The amount of debt a company carries on its books in relation to equity in the firm.

liability: A debt or obligation.

LIFO (Last In/First Out): A method for valuing inventory that assumes the last product manufactured is the first one sold. [See: FIFO.]

line method: A system of inventory control that relies on placing products in a container with a line drawn around it—usually about a third of the way up from the bottom. When the merchandise reaches that line, it is time to reorder.

line of credit: A loan with an established limit that gives a company access to money but only charges interest on the money actually borrowed.

liquidity: The ability to convert assets to cash.

local clearinghouse: Networks of banks in a particular location that meet daily to physically exchange checks.

lock box: A mailbox administered by a third-party that allows customers to make payments to a location near them that the administrator can post immediately to a local bank account in the company's name.

long-term debt: An obligation to pay a certain amount in a period of time beyond a year. Examples of long-term debt are bank loans, mortgages, and bonds.

macroeconomics: How overall economic forces affect companies and individuals.

made-to-order: Finished goods converted from raw materials after customers place orders for them.

made-to-stock: Finished goods converted from raw materials to be held in inventory before customers place orders for them.

mail float: The time it takes the U.S. Postal Service to deliver a check that's been put in the mail.

managerial accounting: The process of gathering and compiling financial information to assist managers in making decisions concerning products, divisions, and costs.

market value: A measurement of a company's worth determined by what investors are willing to pay for it. This is calculated by multiplying the number of shares of common stock outstanding against the price each share commands in the stock market.

MBA: An academic designation that indicates that the recipient holds a master's degree in business administration.

MDA (multiple discriminant analysis): A method of determining which companies to extend credit to, using a scoring system based on a variety of criteria, including income and debt.

money-market mutual fund: A mutual fund that invests in short-term, low-risk securities such as Treasury bills, commercial paper, and certificates of deposit which enables investors to immediately liquidate their holdings.

mortgage-backed bonds: A secured debt instrument that uses real estate as collateral.

municipal bond: Debt security issued by state and local governments that is free of federal taxes and may be exempt from state taxes if the purchaser resides in the issuing state.

Nasdaq Composite Index: A measurement of the performance of the U.S. stock market based on the prices of certain select over-the-counter stocks.

net income: [See: profit.]

net margin: A measurement of a company's profit calculated by dividing net income by net sales. [See: profit margin.]

net worth: The measure of the owner's investment in a company. It is also the amount by which a company's assets exceed liabilities.

non-notification factoring: A factoring arrangement whereby a company repays a factor based on receivables collected.

notification basis factoring: A factoring arrangement whereby a company's customers pay the factor directly when they purchase products.

operating budgets: Sales and expense budgets that reflect information found on the income statement detailing business operations for a specific period of time.

operating income: The item on an income statement calculated by subtracting indirect costs from gross income.

operating margin: A measurement of a company's management of indirect costs calculated by dividing operating income by net sales.

ordering costs: The administrative expenses, such as the costs of processing invoices and taking delivery, that a company incurs when it places an order for inventory.

P&L (profit and loss) statement: [See: income statement.]

Pareto's Law: Also known as the 80/20 rule: the principle that 80 percent of a company's output is derived from 20 percent of its input.

partnership: A business owned by two or more persons, each of whom according to the IRS, "contributes money, property, labor, or skill, and expects to share in the profits and losses of the business."

perpetual inventory control: A system of keeping track of inventory on a continuous basis so management knows at all times how much inventory is in stock.

PPI (producer price index): A measurement of inflation based on the changes in the wholesale price of goods sold to businesses.

preferred stock: A type of stock that entitles the holder to receive fixed dividends. Preferred stockholders have no voting rights in the corporation.

privately held corporation: A company that does not sell stock to the general public.

private placement: A sale of stock without a public offering.

processing float: The time it takes a company's collection department or lock box administrator to sort through payment envelopes, record vital information, and deposit checks with the Federal Reserve processing center or local clearinghouse.

profit: Income after expenses have been deducted.

profit center: Segment of a company that is responsible for generating profit on its own.

profit margin: A measure of a company's profitability calculated by dividing the net income by net sales. [See: net margin.]

publicly traded company: A company that sells its stock to the public.

quick ratio: A measurement of a company's ability to pay its short-term debt calculated by dividing current assets minus inventory by current liabilities.

R&D (research & development): The process by which a company creates and brings new products to market or improves existing products.

raw materials: Materials a company uses to manufacture its products.

recession: A period of declining economic activity.

remote disbursement: A method of payment, declared by the Federal Reserve to be abusive, that strategically issues a payment to a vendor from an account located in a different state. The purpose of remote disbursement is to delay a vendor's access to the funds.

replacement cost valuation: A method of valuing an asset based on how much it costs to buy a new one.

retained earnings: Profits that are reinvested into the company.

risk: The measure of a company's long-term solvency.

ROA (return on assets): A measurement of how efficiently a company has used its assets to generate profit. It is calculated by dividing net income by total assets.

ROE (return on equity): A measurement of a company's profitability calculated by dividing net income by shareholder equity.

ROI (return on investment): A measurement of the return a company has generated on the owners' investments.

Rule of Three: The principle that divides a company (or its departments) into three parts: one part that is considered essential, another part that is desirable, and a third part that is dispensable.

safety stock: A surplus of finished goods that serves as protection, should there be delays in inventory delivery or as replacement for damaged merchandise.

sales budget: A planning document that projects sales.

S & P 500 (Standard & Poor's) Stock Index: A market-value-weighted index of 500 companies traded on the New York Stock Exchange, the American Stock Exchange, and over-the-counter that serves as a proxy for the performance of U.S. stocks.

SEC (Securities and Exchange Commission): The regulatory agency of the federal government that administers securities laws and oversees the securities markets.

secured loan: A debt that requires collateral.

self-employment taxes: Taxes paid by self-employed individuals for Social Security and Medicare.

share buyback: An arrangement whereby a company repurchases its own shares of stock on the open market.

short-term financing: Loans and credit that must be repaid within a year.

sole proprietorship: An unincorporated company owned by a single individual.

solvency: The ability of a company to meet its financial obligations.

statement of cash flows: [See: cash flow statement.]

static budget: A budget that is prepared at the beginning of the year and remains unchanged until the end of the year.

stock: A share of ownership in a corporation.

straight-line depreciation: A method of calculating an asset's loss of value by dividing the number of years of its useful life into its historic cost, and depreciating the resulting sum equally over its life expectancy.

Subchapter-S corporation: A corporation with 75 or fewer shareholders which operates as a corporation but gets taxed as a partnership.

subordinated debenture: A long-term debt instrument that generally offers a higher interest rate than a straight debenture, because in the event of bankruptcy, the holders cannot make claims on the company's assets until after the other creditors recoup their money.

supply and demand: An understanding of economics in which prices rise when demand outstrips supply, and prices fall when supply outstrips demand.

T-account: A visual device with two columns that allows accountants to record transactions accurately.

taxable income: Amount of a company's income that is subject to taxation. It is generally net income before taxes.

10-K: An annual financial report required of publicly traded companies that is filed with the SEC.

10-Q: A quarterly financial report required of publicly traded companies that is filed with the SEC.

total inventory costs: Carrying costs plus ordering costs.

treasurer: The person responsible for raising, spending, investing, and managing the company's assets.

two-bin method: A system of keeping track of inventory that uses two separate bins to hold the merchandise. When the first bin is emptied, it is time to reorder.

ultra-short-term bond fund: A mutual fund that invests in extremely short-term bonds allowing investors to immediately liquidate their holdings.

unsecured loan: A debt that does not require collateral.

U.S. Treasury bill: A safe, short-term debt security of the U.S. Treasury that typically matures in three months to a year.

U.S. Treasury bond: A long-term debt security of the U.S. Treasury that typically matures in 10 to 30 years.

U.S. Treasury note: An intermediate-term debt security of the U.S. Treasury that typically matures in three to ten years.

variable expenses: Costs of doing business that rise and fall depending on the volume of products made or sold.

variance: The difference between actual and budgeted numbers.

venture capital: Source of financing for startups.

ZBA (zero balance account): A type of checking account used for disbursing payments that maintains a $0 balance. It is used to centralize the disbursement process and to ensure that excess cash can be invested on a daily basis.

RESOURCES

Books.

1993 International Investors Directory. Eric Laursen and Charles Ruffel, eds. (Asset International, 1993).

1997 International Tax Summaries: A Guide for Planning and Decisions. George J. Yost, III, ed., Coopers, Lybrand Global Tax Network, and David Benson (John Wiley & Sons, 1997)

The ABCs of International Finance. John Charles Pool (Lexington Books, 1991).

Accounting. Charles T. Horngren, Walter T. Harrison Jr. and Michael A. Robinson (Prentice Hall, 1996).

Accounting and Finance for Nonspecialists. Peter Atrill and Eddie McLaney (Prentice Hall, 1997).

Accounting for the New Business: The Strategies and Practices You Need to Account for Your Success. Christopher R. Malburg (Adams Publishing, 1997).

Accounting Handbook. Joel G. Siegel and Jae K. Shim (Barron's Educational Series, 1995).

Accounting: The Basis for Business Decisions (10th edition). Robert F. Meigs, Mary A. Meigs, Mark Bettner and Ray Whittington (McGraw-Hill Text, 1996).

Accounting the Easy Way. Peter J. Eisen (Barron's Educational Series, 1995).

The Blackwell Encyclopedic Dictionary of Accounting (Blackwell Encyclopedia of Management). Rashad Abdel-Khalik, ed. (Blackwell Publishing, 1997).

Corporate Controller's Manual 1997. Paul J. Wendell (Warren, Gorham & Lamont, 1996).

Corporate Finance Sourcebook 1998. (National Register Publishing Company, 1997).

A Dictionary of Accounting. R. Hussey, ed. (Oxford University Press Trade, 1996).

Dictionary of Accounting Terms. Joel G. Siegel and Jae K. Shim (Barron's Educational Series, 1995).

Dictionary of Finance and Investment Terms. John Downes and Jordan Elliot Goodman (Barron's Educational Series, 1995).

Ernst & Young Tax Saver's Guide 1998. Ernst, Young, Peter W. Bernstein, ed. (John Wiley & Sons, 1997).

Essentials of Accounting. Robert N. Anthony (Addison-Wesley Publishing, 1996).

Essentials of Managerial Finance (11th Edition). J. Fred Weston, Scott Besley, and Eugene F. Brigham (The Dryden Press, 1996).

Finance & Accounting for Nonfinancial Managers: All the Basics You Need to Know. William G. Droms (Addison Wesley Publishing Company, 1998).

Finance: Barron's EZ-101 Study Keys. Joel G. Siegel and Jae K. Shim (Barron's Educational Series, 1991).

Financial Accounting Theory. William R. Scott (Prentice Hall, 1996).

The Guide to Understanding Financial Statements. S. B. Costales and Geza Azurovy (McGraw-Hill, 1993).

Managerial Accounting. Arthur J. Francia, ed. (Dame Publications, 1994).

Market Movers. Nancy Dunnand and Jay Pack (Warner Books, 1993).

The McGraw-Hill 36-Hour Course in Finance for Nonfinancial Managers. Robert A. Cooke (McGraw-Hill, 1993).

The Portable MBA Tool Kit in Finance and Accounting. John Tracy (John Wiley & Sons, 1995).

Understanding Cash Flow (Finance Fundamentals for Nonfinancial Managers). Franklin J. Plewa and George T. Friedlob (John Wiley & Sons, 1995).

Magazines, Newspapers, and Other Publications

Accounting Today. 11 Penn Plaza, New York, NY 10001, (212) 967-7060, $82.95/yr., (semimonthly).

Barron's. 200 Liberty St., New York, NY 10281, (800) 568-7625, $145/yr., (weekly).

BusinessWeek. 1221 Avenue of the Americas, New York, NY 10020, (800) 635-1200, $49.95/yr., (weekly).

Financial World. 1328 Broadway, New York, NY 10001, (800) 829-5916, $27/yr., (18 issues).

Forbes. 60 Fifth Ave., New York, NY 10011, (800) 888-9896, $59.95/yr., (biweekly).

Fortune. P.O. Box 60001, Tampa, FL 33660, (800) 621-8000, $57/yr., (biweekly).

Global Custodian. 125 Greenwich Ave., Greenwich, CT 06830, (203) 629-5014, fax: (203) 629-5024, e-mail: office@assetpub.com, $80/yr., (quarterly).

Hulbert Financial Digest. 316 Commerce St., Alexandria, VA 22314, (703) 683-5905, $59/yr., (monthly).

Institutional Investor. 488 Madison Ave., New York, NY 10022, (212) 224-3570, $425/yr., (monthly).

Investor's Business Daily. 12655 Beatrice St., Los Angeles, CA 90066, (800) 831-2525, $189/yr., (daily).

Journal of Accountancy. 1211 Avenue of the Americas, New York, NY 10036, (800) 862-4272, e-mail: journal@aicpa.org, $56/yr. (free to AICPA members), (monthly).

Nation's Business. 1615 H St. NW, Washington, DC 20062, (202) 463-5434, e-mail: ireadnb@nationsbusiness.org, $22/yr., (monthly).

Pensions & Investments. 965 East Jefferson Ave., Detroit, MI 48238, (800) 678-9595, $205/yr., (biweekly).

Plan Sponsor. 125 Greenwich Ave., Greenwich, CT. 06830, (203) 629-5014, fax: (203) 629-5024, e-mail: office@assetpub.com, $150/yr. (free to finance and accounting professionals), (10 issues).

The Wall Street Journal. 200 Liberty St., New York, NY 10281, (800) 568-7625, $175/yr., (daily, Monday through Friday).

Worth. P.O. Box 55420, Boulder, CO 80323, (800) 727-9098, $18/yr., (monthly, 10 issues).

Online Resources

Asset International Web site, http://www.assetpub.com/product.html

Bloomberg Web site, http://www.bloomberg.com

Federal Trade Commission Web site, http://www.ftc.gov

Financenter Web site, http://www.financenter.com

Internal Revenue Service Web site, http://www.irs.ustreas.gov

PAWWS Financial Network Web site, http://www.pawws.secapl.com

Quicken Financial Network Web site, http://www.qfn.com/index.html

Securities and Exchange Commission Web site, http://www.sec.gov

U.S. Investor Network Web site, http://www.usinvestor.com

Associations and Organizations

AICPA (American Institute of Certified Public Accountants). 1211 Avenue of the Americas, New York, NY 10036, (212) 596-6200, fax: (212) 596-6213, Web site: http://www.aicpa.org/

Dun & Bradstreet. 899 Eaton Ave., Bethlehem, PA 18025, (800) 234-3867, Web site: http://www.dbisna.com/dbis/purchase/tpurchase.htm

Internal Revenue Service. Department of the Treasury, 12th St. and Constitution Ave., Washington, DC 20210, (202) 829-1040, Web site: http://www.irs.ustreas.gov

National Center for Financial Education. P.O. Box 34070, San Diego, CA 92163, (619) 232-8811.

Securities Data. 2 Gateway Center, Newark, NJ 07102, (973) 622-3100.

Securities and Exchange Commission. 450 Fifth St. NW, Washington, DC 20549, (202) 942-7040, Web site: http://www.sec.gov

U.S. Department of Agriculture. 14th St. and Independence Ave. SW, Washington, DC 20250, (202) 720-2791, Web site: http://www.usda.gov/about.htm

U.S. Department of Commerce. 14th St. and Constitution Ave. NW, Room 5327, Washington, DC 20230, (202) 482-2000, Web site: http://www.OSEC.doc.gov/OS/

U.S. Department of Labor. 200 Constitution Ave. NW, Washington, DC 20210, (202) 219-8211, Web site: http://www.dol.gov

INDEX

accountants, 3, 5, 10, 11, 13, 44, 49
   controller, 10, 12; cost, 11–13, 120;
   tax, 10–13

accounting, 3–5
   accrual, 20, 21, 115; cost, 110–113,
   120; financial, 13, 18, 19, 21,
   111–113; managerial, 14, 18, 19,
   21

accounts payable, 22, 24, 25, 29, 31, 32, 34, 35,
   40, 63, 65, 70, 73, 86, 124, 129–131, 182

accounts receivable, 20, 22–25, 31–34, 40, 61, 62,
   70, 73, 86, 129, 133, 135, 137, 146, 149,
   151–153, 184–186

accrual accounting, 20–22, 40, 43, 71, 93

ACH (automated clearinghouse network), 134

activity-based costing, 120

Advice to a Young Tradesman, 130

AICPA (American Institute of Certified Public
   Accountants), 127

Alcoa, 207

Allied Signal, 207

Almanac of Business and Industrial Ratios, 78

American Express, 207

American Institute of Certified Public Accountants,
   2

American Stock Exchange, 192, 206

amortization, 47, 58, 59, 62, 64, 65, 73, 74
   accumulated, 70; straight line
   method of, 47

annual reports, 11, 68, 69

Annual Statement Studies, 78

APB (Accounting Principles Board), 22

appreciation, 47, 201

assets, 1, 2, 5, 13, 14, 20, 24–26, 37, 55, 57, 62,
   66, 70–74, 82, 84, 189
   accounting for, 12, 56; accounts
   receivable, 20, 22–25, 31–34, 40,
   61, 62, 70, 73; balance sheets, 61,
   62, 65, 71; buildings, 64; cash, 1, 2,
   3, 5, 6, 7, 14–16, 19–23, 25, 26,
   28, 31–34, 39, 40, 42, 44, 60–62,
   70–75, 77, 83, 85, 86–88 90, 93,
   94, 97–99, 101, 123–126,
   128–131, 139–143 ; converting to
   cash, 6, 61, 73, 83; copyrights, 20,
   47, 64, 65; corporate, 176; credit,
   21, 29, 39, 40, 61, 93, 124, 129,
   138, 143; current, 20, 23, 61, 62,
   83–85, 128, 130, 184; depreciation
   of, 38, 46–52, 65; equipment, 23,
   64, 96; factories, 20; fixed, 20, 64,
   73, 96, 124, 186, 187; goodwill,
   20, 47, 64; historic cost of, 51;
   inventory, 20, 29, 37, 38, 64, 72,
   73, 115, 156; liquid, 124; long-
   term, 97; managing, 7, 12, 85; measuring, 44; net worth, 23; noncurrent, 23; paper, 21, 40; patents, 20,
   47, 64, 65; property, 23; real estate,

20; ROA (return on assets), 83;
ROI (return on investment), 80, 81;
sole proprietorships, 174; T-
accounts, 27, 28, 30, 32–34; track-
ing, 127; write-offs, 68, 82
AT&T, 207
auditing, 69
    financial accounting statements, 19;
    internal, 11–13

balance sheets, 5, 14, 19, 21, 59, 61–68, 71–73,
    75, 77, 78, 88, 90, 101, 115, 148, 194
bank, 3
    accounts, 25, 39, 60, 133, 136, 139;
    clearinghouses, 134–136; credit
    cards, 39; electronic transfers, 134,
    139; failures, 193; Federal Reserve,
    105, 120, 131, 132, 135, 136, 139,
    196, 198, 204; investment, 15; lines
    of credit, 124, 183, 185; loans, 23,
    125, 181, 182, 186; mortgages, 55,
    188, 198; statements, 142; ZBA
    (zero balance account), 139

bankruptcy, 189, 191, 199
bear market, 196, 209, 210
Bethlehem Steel, 207
Black Tuesday, 193
board of directors, 9, 13, 68, 140, 178, 192
Boeing, 207
Bollenbach, Stephen, 11
bonds, 60, 124–126, 188, 189, 191, 196, 205, 210
    convertible, 189; corporate, 143,
    205; debentures, 189; funds, 141;
    interest on, 143, 189; investment
    grade, 140, 189, 190, 205; junk,
    189, 190, 205; maturity date, 189;
    Moody's Investor Service, 190;
    mortgage-backed, 189, 205; munici-
    pal, 143; ratings, 190, 191; risk,
    189; Standard & Poor's, 190;
    Treasury, 142; yields, 196, 198

book value, 61
bottom line, 4, 59, 60
break-even, 106, 107, 109
    by sales, 108; by units, 108
buildings, 62, 64
    depreciation of, 47, 65
budgets, 4, 6, 13, 86–90, 194
    advertising, 93; annual, 127; assem-
    bling, 99–101; bottom-up, 100;
    break-even point, 106–109; cash,
    87, 93, 94, 101, 128, 140, 170;
    capital, 6, 10–13, 90, 95, 97–99;
    contribution margin, 107, 108;
    earnings, 87; expense, 6, 87, 93,
    106; flexible, 95–97; forecasts, 6;
    general & administrative, 93, 102;
    historic performance data, 101, 102;
    incremental, 103, 104; industry
    trends, 104; inventory, 91; IRR
    (internal rate of return), 99; market-
    ing, 90; master, 90, 93; net present
    value analysis, 98, 99; officers,
    10–12; payback analysis, 97, 98;
    projections, 93, 95, 103, 105, 106;
    R & D (research & development),
    93, 102; rent, 93; revenue, 97, 101;
    Rule of Three, 90; sales, 6, 87, 93,
    95, 97, 102–105; static, 93; tax, 94,
    96; top-down, 100; variances, 93,
    95; zero-based, 103, 104
bull market, 209, 210
Bureau of Alcohol, Tobacco, and Firearms, 172

CAP (Committee on Accounting Procedure), 22
capital, 84, 85, 148
    borrowed, 182; budgets, 6, 10–13,
    90, 95, 97–99; working, 126, 128,
    140

Capital Cities/ABC, 11
    Bollenbach, Stephen, 11

cash, 1, 23, 25, 31, 40, 62, 70, 73–75, 86, 123, 125, 130
  basis accounting, 39, 40, 42; budgets, 6, 90, 93, 94, 128, 140, 170; conversion cycles, 129, 130; converting assets to, 6, 20, 23, 61, 83; equivalents, 61, 62, 70, 75, 85, 125, 140; excess, 126; flow, 2, 5, 6, 14, 19, 21, 44, 70–75, 77, 86–88, 90, 93, 94, 97–99, 101, 123, 126, 128, 131, 140, 141, 149, 159, 170, 183, 184, 188; investing, 2, 3, 15, 60, 126, 139–143, 181; liquidity, 6, 16; managing, 7, 14, 15, 86, 123, 126, 140, 146, 151; projections, 141; spending, 22; T-accounts, 28, 32–34

Caterpillar, 207
CDs (certificates of deposit), 141
CEOs (chief executive officers), 9, 11, 13, 14, 68
CFOs (chief financial officers), 9–11, 13–15
  Bollenbach, Stephen, 11; Invester, Doug, 11

checking accounts, 25, 27, 39
Chevron, 207
clearinghouses ACH (automated clearinghouse network), 134; local, 135, 136
Coca-Cola, 207
  Ivester, Doug, 11

collateral, 55, 148, 184
collecting payments, 130, 132, 136, 140, 145, 146
  collection agencies, 150, 186; cost of, 149; credit cards, 133; delinquent accounts, 150, 152; depository transfer checks, 135; electronic transfers, 134; factors, 186; float, 131–134; incentives, 133, 153; invoicing, 132, 133; late payments, 133; lock boxes, 134–138; preauthorized payments, 133

commercial paper, 185
comptrollers [see controllers]
conditional sales contract, 147

Conference Board, 199
consumer confidence, 105, 194, 196, 199, 200, 206, 210
contribution margin, 107, 108, 119
controllers, 10–14
copyrights, 20, 64, 65
corporations, 178
  taxes, 170, 173, 174, 176–179

cost, 115
  accounting, 110–113, 116; controlling, 123; current, 46; direct, 79, 88, 89, 102; exit, 46; fixed, 117–120; indirect, 59, 80, 89, 91, 102; job, 114, 116–118; labor, 57, 116, 121; opportunity, 126; process, 114, 117, 118; product, 113; raw materials, 57; reducing, 119; replacement cost, 46; shared, 120, 121; shipping, 57; standard, 118–120; unit, 113, 114, 116; variable, 91, 97, 103, 106, 107, 109, 110, 117–119

CPAs (certified public accountants), 69
CPI (consumer price index), 201, 203, 204
credit, 29, 39, 40, 61, 93, 143, 146, 153
  cards, 133, 139, 151, 185, 198; conditional sales contract, 147; costs of, 149; delinquent accounts, 150, 152; Five C's of, 147; lines of, 124, 183, 185; loose, 15, 146, 148, 151; managers, 10–13; managing, 7, 14, 15, 145, 146; MDA (multiple discriminant analysis), 146, 147; outstanding, 152; rating, 125, 138, 140, 185, 189; reports, 148; revolving, 151, 185; scoring system, 147; standards, 146; T-accounts, 27–35; terms, 146, 147; tight, 15, 146, 151; trade, 21, 124, 129, 138, 146, 153, 182, 184

currency trends, 105
  exchange rates, 105

current ratio, 83–85, 128, 131
cycle of finance, 3–5, 9, 10

days payable ratio, 86
debit cards, 27
  T-accounts, 27–35
debt, 65, 82, 148
  collateral, 148; collecting, 15, 150,
  151; current ratio, 83; delinquent,
  150, 152; financing, 15; intermediate-term, 74; leverage, 182, 183;
  loans, 22; long-term, 63, 65, 66, 70,
  74, 75, 84, 85, 124, 125, 187–189;
  past due, 152; ratios, 83–85; short-
  term, 72, 74, 189
deflation, 183, 193, 201
depository transfer checks, 135
depreciation, 38, 44, 46, 47, 50–53, 58, 59, 73,
  74, 89, 93, 102, 201
  accelerated, 48–50; accumulated,
  62, 64, 70, 73; buildings, 47, 64;
  double-declining balance, 49; equipment, 47, 48, 64, 65; of intangible
  assets, 65; machinery, 47; plant, 65;
  property, 65; straight-line, 48, 49,
  51–53; sum-of-the-years rule,
  50–53; taxes, 52
dividends, 66, 67, 70, 75, 191
  T-accounts, 27; taxes on, 178
double-declining balance, 49
double–entry system, 24, 26, 28
  credit, 27; debit, 27; T-accounts, 27
Dow, Charles, 205
Dow Jones Company, 205
Dow Jones Industrial Average, 205–207
downsizing, 200
DSO (days sales outstanding), 84, 86, 126, 129,
  130, 146, 151
Dun & Bradstreet, 104, 148, 199
DuPont, 207

earnings, 4, 6, 13, 19, 56, 68, 77, 82, 112, 169,
  183

budgets, 87; projections, 88; rein-
  vesting, 75, 81; retained, 63, 66–68;
  sole proprietorships, 174, 176
Eastman Kodak, 207
Edwards Directory of American Factors, 186
employees, 3, 30
  hiring, 1, 2, 22, 142; payroll, 2, 3,
  30, 33
engineering, 9
EOQ (economic ordering quantity), 161, 162
Equifax, 148
equipment, 23, 25, 70, 74, 121
  balance sheet entry, 62, 64; depreciation of, 47, 48, 65; T-accounts, 28;
  purchases, 93
equity
  debt-to-equity ratio, 84; financing,
  15, 191; investors, 15; private placements, 15, 191; public offerings, 15,
  191, 210; ROE (return on equity),
  81, 83; share buybacks, 142; shareholder, 20, 23, 24, 26, 61, 63, 66,
  67, 81, 82, 84; venture capital, 192
exchange rates, 105
expansion, 125
expenses, 1, 2, 5, 12, 13, 26, 52, 55–57, 59, 94, 96,
  97, 109, 115
  accrual basis accounting, 40, 43, 71;
  amortization, 59, 64; bonuses, 59;
  budgets, 6; cash basis accounting,
  43; consulting fees, 59; depreciation, 58, 59, 64, 102; distribution,
  91; divisional, 18; general & administrative, 58, 59, 89, 91, 94, 102,
  103; historic data, 102; inflation,
  105; insurance, 91, 106; interest,
  58, 60; managing, 7, 14; payroll,
  65; production, 91; projections, 88,
  100; R & D (research & development), 59, 91, 93, 94; reports, 127;
  sales, 58, 59, 89, 91, 94, 102; T-
  accounts, 27; travel, 59

Exxon, 208

factories, 20, 118, 120, 121
factors, 185–188
   *Edwards Directory of American
   Factors,* 186
FASB (Financial Accounting Standards Board), 20,
   22
Federal Reserve Bank, 105, 120, 131, 132, 135,
   136, 139, 196, 198, 204
FICA (Federal Insurance Contributions Act), [see
   Social Security]
FIFO (first in, first out), 41–45
financial accounting, 13, 18, 19, 21, 111–113
   standards, 19; statements, 19
financial officers, 7
financial ratios, 6, 77–87, 101, 104, 128, 131, 147
financial statements, 4, 6, 14, 21, 44, 47, 52, 68,
   87, 104, 148
   10-K reports, 104, 192; 10-Q
   reports, 104, 192; annual reports,
   11, 68, 69, 104; balance sheets, 5,
   61, 68, 88, 101, 115, 148, 194;
   cash flow statements, 5, 6, 68, 70,
   71, 73, 74, 77, 90, 101, 131; historic performance data, 101; horizontal analysis of, 57; income statements, 5, 6, 14, 19, 40, 47, 48,
   50–52, 56, 58–61, 64, 71, 72, 77,
   78, 80, 88, 101, 117, 148, 150,
   194; projected, 93; reconciliation of
   net worth statement, 67; retained
   earnings statements, 68; vertical
   analysis of, 57
financing, 1, 7, 14, 15, 74, 181, 182, 194
   bonds, 60, 124–126, 143, 188, 189;
   bridge, 189; cash flow from, 70–72,
   74, 75, 131; debt, 15, 60, 70, 74,
   84; debt-to-equity ratio, 84; equity,
   15, 183, 190; expansion, 125, 182;
   factors, 185–188; intermediate-term
   loans, 183, 186, 189; inventory,
   185; leasing, 191; lines of credit,

124, 183, 185; long-term, 66, 188,
   192; mortgages, 55, 188, 189, 198;
   short-term, 183–185, 189; venture
   capital, 192
float, 131–134, 138, 139
forecasts, 6
Fortune, 11
Fortune 100, 129
Francia, Arthur J., 111
Franklin, Benjamin, 130
fraud, 142
FUTA (Federal Unemployment Tax Act), 172

GAAP (generally accepted accounting principles),
   19–21, 44, 47, 52, 64, 115
   APB (Accounting Principles Board),
   22; CAP (Committee on
   Accounting Procedure), 22; FASB
   (Financial Accounting Standards
   Board), 20, 22; IRS (Internal
   Revenue Service), 20
Galbraith, John Kenneth, 193, 199
GDP (gross domestic product), 194–200, 206
General Electric, 208
General Motors, 208
GNP (gross national product), 195
goodwill, 20, 64
Goodyear, 208
Great Depression, 193, 196, 209

Hewlett-Packard, 208
Hilton Hotels, 11
   Bollenbach, Stephen, 11
historic cost valuation, 44, 51, 64
historic performance data, 101
   expenses, 102; sales, 101
hurdle rate, 99

IBM, 208
income, 81
   gross, 58, 59, 78, 174; interest, 58,
   60; net, 4, 58, 60, 66, 67, 70, 72,

73, 80–82; operating, 58, 59, 80, 88, 89, 97; pretax, 58, 60; statements, 5, 6, 14, 19, 21, 40, 47, 48, 50–52, 56, 58–60, 64, 65, 68, 71, 72, 77, 78, 80, 88, 101, 115, 148, 150, 194; taxes, 58, 60, 169, 174–177

Index of Leading Economic Indicators, 199
Industry Norms and Key Business Ratios, 78
inflation, 7, 41, 42, 103, 105, 158, 183, 194–196, 199–202, 204, 206, 210
insurance, 16
Intel, 85, 160, 205
interest, 145, 146, 149, 182
    bond, 143, 189; expense, 58, 60, 174; income, 58, 60, 98, 131; rates, 7, 105, 124–126, 133, 183, 185–188, 194, 196, 198, 199, 204–206, 210

International Paper, 208
inventory, 1, 20, 23, 25, 29, 30, 37, 38, 62, 64, 70, 72, 73, 83–85, 113, 115, 128, 130, 143, 145, 149, 152, 160
    budget, 91; control, 165–167; conversion, 128–130; costs of, 161–163; depleting, 40; EOQ (economic ordering quantity), 161–164, excess, 16; FIFO (first in, first out), 42–45; financing, 185; finished goods, 157–159, 163; fluctuations, 199; LIFO (last in, first out), 42, 44, 45; made-to-order, 157; made-to-stock, 158; managers, 10–13; managing, 7, 14, 15, 155, 156, 159, 164, 165; ordering, 160, 161, 165–167; overstocking, 25, 156, 159, 163; raw materials, 57, 156, 158, 159, 202; retail, 188; safety stock, 163; site specific, 18; T-accounts, 31, 34; turnover, 84, 85, 128; understocking, 16, 156, 160;

valuation methods of, 41, 45; work in progress, 156, 159
investing, 2–4, 11, 19, 21, 42, 67, 82, 98, 125, 182, 193
    American Stock Exchange, 192; annual reports, 11, 68; bank accounts, 60; bear market, 196; bonds, 60, 126, 140–143, 188, 189, 196, 198, 205; cash, 15, 60, 126, 131, 132, 139–141, 181; cash flow from, 70, 71, 73, 74, 131, 141, 142; CDs (certificates of deposit), 141; current ratio, 83; debt, 82; dividends, 170; earnings, 75, 81; hurdle rate, 99; interest rates, 125; long-term projects, 97; market value, 61; money market funds, 60, 141; Nasdaq, 192; net worth, 66; New York Stock Exchange, 192; quick ratio, 83; rate of return, 2, 3; risk tolerance, 140; ROI (return on investment), 80, 82, 126; SEC (Security and Exchange Commission), 19, 21, 68, 69, 104; share buybacks, 142; stocks, 60, 61, 72, 126, 142, 181, 182, 189, 191, 196, 198, 210; Treasury bills, 140; Treasury bonds, 142; Treasury notes, 142; venture capital, 192

invoices, 127, 132, 133
IPOs (initial public offerings), 210
IRR (internal rate of return), 99
IRS (Internal Revenue Service), 19, 20, 43, 170, 171, 174. 175, 179, 195
    depreciation, 48, 49, 51, 52; forms, 172, 174–176; publications, 178; Web site, 178

Ivester, Doug, 11

J. P. Morgan, 208
job order sheet, 116, 117

Johnson & Johnson, 208
joint ventures, 175, 182

Keynes, John Maynard, 6
KPMG Peat Marwick, 159

labor, 116, 117, 119
    cost of, 57, 116, 120, 121, 124;
    strikes, 125
land, 62, 64, 124
ledgers, 23–25, 39
    T-accounts, 26–28, 30, 31, 33, 40
Lehman Brothers Aggregate Bond Index, 205
leverage, 182, 183
liabilities, 2, 5, 13, 20, 22, 25, 26, 56, 57, 66,
    71–73, 82, 84
    accounts payable, 22, 24, 25, 29,
    31, 32, 34, 35, 40, 63, 65, 70, 73;
    accrued payroll, 63, 65, 70, 73; bal-
    ance sheets, 61, 63, 71; current, 22,
    23, 63, 65, 83–85, 128, 131; debt,
    15, 22–24, 65, 72, 74; limited, 176;
    long-term, 22, 23, 65, 66; manag-
    ing, 7, 12, 14; net worth, 23; non-
    current, 23; paper, 22, 40; partner-
    ships, 175; salary, 22, 23; sole pro-
    prietorships, 175; Subchapter-S cor-
    porations, 179; T-accounts, 27,
    29–33, 35; wages, 23
licenses, 93
LIFO (last in, first out), 41–45
liquidity, 6, 16, 56, 78, 128, 141
    accounts receivable, 61; assets, 20,
    46, 64; cash, 61; of inventory, 159;
    measuring, 83, 131; ratios, 83, 84,
    131
loans, 22, 131
    bridge financing, 189; bank, 23, 55,
    188; car, 198; collateral, 55, 148,
    184; compensating balances, 184;
    defaults on, 149; intermediate-term,
    183, 186, 189; long-term, 66, 188;

mortgages, 55, 189, 198; secured,
    184, 189; short-term, 184, 189;
    unsecured, 184, 189; venture capi-
    tal, 192
lock boxes, 134–138

machinery, 62, 64
    depreciation of, 47
macroeconomics, 105, 194
    consumer confidence, 105, 194,
    196, 199, 200, 206, 210; deflation,
    183, 193, 201; economic growth,
    194–201, 206, 210; Great
    Depression, 193, 196, 209; infla-
    tion, 7, 41, 42, 103, 105, 158, 183,
    194–196, 199–202, 204, 206, 210;
    interest rates, 7, 105, 124–126, 133,
    183, 185–188, 194, 196, 198, 206,
    210; recession, 105, 195, 196, 200,
    209; unemployment, 193, 194, 199,
    200, 210
managerial
    accounting, 14, 18, 19, 21; reports,
    18, 19, 88, 101
Managerial Accounting, 111
managers
    credit, 10–13; inventory, 10–13;
    plant, 12; sales, 13
markdowns, 159
market value, 61
marketing, 124
    budgets, 90
Marriott
    Bollenbach, Stephen, 11
MBA (Masters degree in business administration)
    Wharton School, 14
McDonald's, 208
MDA (multiple discriminant analysis), 146, 147
Medicare
    taxes, 171, 172

Merck, 208
mergers and acquisitions, 126
Microsoft, 181, 205
Minnesota Mining & Manufacturing, 208
Money Magazine, 151
money market funds, 60, 141
Moody's Investor Service, 190
mortgages, 55, 188, 189, 198

Nasdaq, 192, 205, 206
near-cash investments, 124
net present value analysis, 98, 99
net worth, 23, 25, 66, 67, 71–73, 75, 84
    book value, 61; calculating, 23, 26;
    reconciliation statement, 75; T-
    accounts, 27
New York Stock Exchange, 192, 206

operating cycles, 29
outsourcing, 114, 167
overhead, 80, 113, 116, 117, 120, 121, 124
organization charts, 9, 10, 13

Pareto's Law, 91
partnerships, 170, 171, 175
    joint ventures, 175, 182; syndicates,
    175; taxes, 173–175, 178, 179
patents, 20, 64, 65, 176
payback analysis, 97, 98
payroll, 2, 15, 124
    accrued, 63, 65, 70, 73; checks, 2,
    3, 124, 127, 170; software, 2; taxes,
    93
Pentium, 160
Philip Morris, 208
PPI (producer price index), 202
prime rate, 185
private placements, 15, 191
Procter & Gamble, 208
product costs, 113
profits, 4, 6, 16, 41, 42, 49, 51, 52, 67, 78, 81, 82,
    88, 105–107, 109, 110, 112, 114, 121, 123,

    149, 169, 170
    bottom line, 4, 59, 60; centers, 4,
    100; FIFO (first in, first out), 43,
    44; gross, 42, 44, 59, 78, 88, 89,
    91, 174; inflated, 41; LIFO (last in,
    first out), 44; margin, 43, 78–80,
    83, 112; measuring, 56; net income,
    4, 58, 60; partnerships, 175, 179;
    ratios, 83; ROA (return on assets),
    83; ROE (return on equity), 82, 83;
    short-term, 5, 41; T-accounts, 34;
    taxes on, 43, 170; total, 59
property, 23, 62, 64, 65, 70, 74
public offerings, 15, 191
    IPOs (initial public offerings), 210
publicly traded companies, 16

quick ratio, 83–85, 128, 131, 147

R & D (research & development), 58, 59
    budgets, 89, 91, 102
raw materials, 29, 31, 124, 156, 158, 159, 202
    converting to inventory, 30, 128,
    129; costs of, 57
real estate, 20
recession, 105, 195, 196, 200, 209
reconciliation of net worth statement, 67, 75
recording transactions, 38–40
remote disbursement, 139
replacement cost, 46
restructurings, 82
revenues, 2, 5, 18, 26, 56, 57, 59, 60, 90, 101, 110
    increasing, 107; net, 107; projected,
    6, 96, 101, 109; T-accounts, 27
risk, 5, 61, 78, 99
    bonds, 189; ratios, 84; tolerance,
    140
ROA (return on assets), 80, 83
ROI (return on investment), 80, 126
ROE (return on equity), 80, 82, 83
running journal, 24